SCIENCE WORKS!

SOUND

STEVE PARKER

MACDONALD YOUNG BOOKS

First published in 1995 by Macdonald Young Books Ltd

© Macdonald Young Books Ltd

Campus 400
Maylands Avenue
Hemel Hempstead
Hertfordshire
HP2 7EZ

Commissioning editor: Thomas Keegan
Designer: Jane Felstead
Editor: Christopher Norris
Illustrators: Maltings Partnership, Chris Lyons,
Martin Woodward, Stephen Mclean, Treve Tamblin
Picture credits: Sally & Richard Greenhill: 35.
The Kobal Collection: 38. Redferns: 4, 21, 33, 44.
Rex Features: 29. Zefa: 6, 9, 10, 13, 14, 17, 36, 40, 42, 45.

A CIP catalogue record for this book is available from the
British Library

ISBN 07500 1594 2

Typeset by Jane Felstead

Printed and bound in Portugal

CONTENTS

SOUND

Hearing is our second most important sense after sight. Our ears let us hear millions of sounds during our lives, but something we never meet is the sound of silence. The world is a noisy place: from wind and rain to the voices that we and many other animals use to communicate, and even the breathing and heartbeats of our own bodies. In our modern world the science of sound – acoustics – has hundreds of uses. It is applied to the design of house walls and concert halls, to the recording of speech and music, and to noise pollution in cities. Sounds bring us information and pleasure, and they can cause stress and pain. They play a central part in daily life.

The story of sound

This book follows ideas about sound, and the way we make and use sounds, from the echoing caves of stone-age times to the modern world of radio, television, compact discs and electronic digital sampling.

The first section of the book examines the nature of sound. What is it? How does it get from one place to another? What do we mean by words such as pitch, frequency and loudness?

The second section looks at sounds in nature, from the whisper of wind in grass to the menacing rumble of thunder, and to the many animals who use sound to hunt prey, repel rivals, frighten enemies, attract mates and care for their babies.

The third section describes the many devices which produce sounds, and how they work. Examples are our voice-boxes (which we use for talking), musical instruments, loudspeakers, and the sonic boom of faster-than-sound aircraft.

The fourth section of the book shows how sounds are detected by a variety of means including the ears of different animals, and microphones in telephones and many other pieces of equipment.

The fifth section describes how inventors and scientists have recorded sounds in different ways, from the wavy groove in a vinyl disc to microscopic pits on a compact disc, and how these sounds are played back again.

The last section looks at some of the more unusual sounds, such as the warning wail of an emergency siren. It also examines how our world seems to be getting steadily noisier.

FAMOUS FIRSTS

Knowledge thrives on 'firsts', such as the person to discover a scientific law or make an invention. The *Famous Firsts* panels describe who got there in front of all the others.

DIY SCIENCE

Follow in the footsteps of well-known scientists by trying the tests and experiments in Do-It-Yourself form, using everyday objects and equipment, as shown in the *DIY Science* panels.

SPECIAL FX

Scientific processes and principles can have fascinating, even startling results. The *Special FX* projects show you how to produce these special effects. Most items are easily available about the home.

WHAT IS SOUND?

We cannot see or feel sound. But our ears tell us that sound is all around. What exactly is a sound and why is it invisible? How does it move and why does it fade away? Scientific research, dating from experiments of the 17th century, has given us most of the answers to the ancient mysteries of sound.

In ancient times people believed that gods above the Earth made the huge sounds for natural events, such as thunderstorms, volcanic eruptions and earthquakes. But early scientists wanted to find out more.

Around 2530 years ago the Greek mathematician Pythagoras observed musical instruments. He saw that when strings of different lengths vibrate, or shake rapidly to and fro, the shorter strings produce higher sounds. Two centuries later Aristotle suggested that sound travelled due to some motion or movement in the air.

During the Dark Ages in Europe there was little progress in science, including the study of sound – acoustics. The revival came in the 17th century, including the invention of the vacuum – a place that contained nothing, not even air.

Further experiments led to the idea that sound travels as

More than 2350 years ago the great Greek thinker and naturalist Aristotle pondered on many problems, including the nature of sound. He believed correctly that it had something to do with invisible movements in air.

SOUND AND THE 'AIR PUMP'

In the 1640s German physicist and engineer Otto von Guericke (1602–1686) modified the water pump into an 'air pump'. It could remove most of the air from a container, leaving almost nothing – a partial vacuum. When a ringing bell was put in the container, and the air was removed, the bell's sound faded away. This was the first good evidence that sound needed something to travel through. English scientists Robert Boyle, Robert Hooke and Francis Hauksbee made better pumps and continued the experiments. In 1705 Hauksbee put a clock in a jar and removed the air, and its ticks went silent.

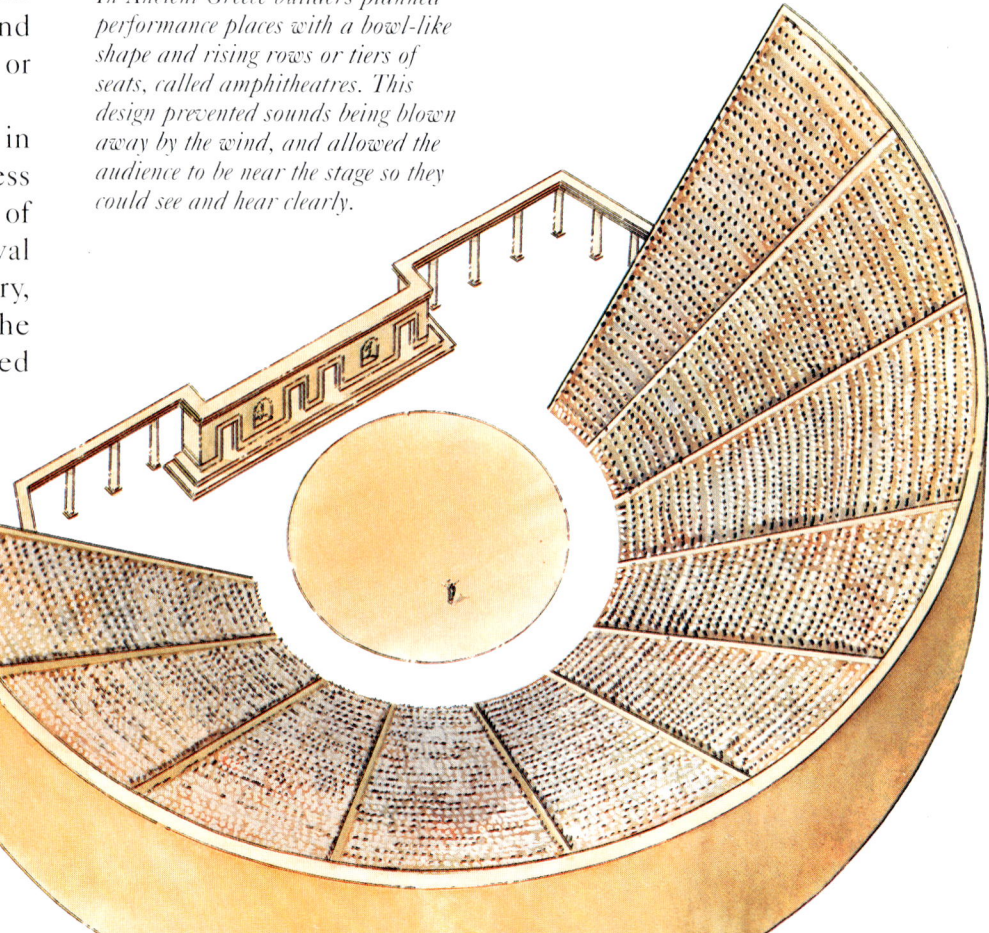

In Ancient Greece builders planned performance places with a bowl-like shape and rising rows or tiers of seats, called amphitheatres. This design prevented sounds being blown away by the wind, and allowed the audience to be near the stage so they could see and hear clearly.

SEEING SOUNDS

Everything in the universe is made up of tiny particles called atoms, either on their own or joined to other atoms to form molecules. Individual atoms and molecules are far too small to see, but when millions of them are clumped together they become visible. This happens in solids where the molecules are close together and held in position so they hardly move. In liquids the molecules are farther apart and can move more easily. In gases they are spaced even farther apart and we cannot see them. Air is a mixture of gas molecules, mainly those of nitrogen and oxygen, with smaller amounts of the rarer atmospheric gases such as argon and carbon dioxide. Sound waves consist of co-ordinated movements or vibrations of these air molecules, in the form of waves of higher and lower air pressure that pass out from the sound source. When these waves arrive at a thin, flexible sheet or membrane, they cause it to shake or vibrate, with visible results.

You need

Plastic bowl, metal baking tray, sheet of very thin and flexible material such as clingfilm or plastic or rubber, large elastic band, wooden spoon, sugar or salt, sticking tape, scissors.

1. Place the sheet over the bowl and pull it to remove creases. Carefully cut the sheet around the bowl, making it about 5 centimetres larger than the bowl.

2. Pull the sheet tightly and evenly over the bowl, and secure it with the elastic band so it is taut like a drum skin.

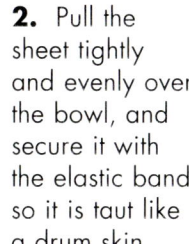

3. Secure the edge of the sheet firmly to the bowl, by using pieces of sticking tape placed at regular intervals.

4. Place some grains of salt or sugar on the taut sheet. Hold the tray nearby and bash it with the spoon.

Sounds bounce and echo in a circle around the Whispering Gallery of St Paul's Cathedral, London.

- In Greek myth Echo, a nymph, kept the goddess Hera talking while her husband Zeus spent time with other women. Hera found out and put a curse on Echo. The nymph could now only repeat what others had said.

- From their rocky island Sirens in Greek legend sang so well that sailors lured towards them were shipwrecked on the rocks.

Bashing the tray produces sound waves in the air.

The sound waves make the thin sheet vibrate and the grains dance about.

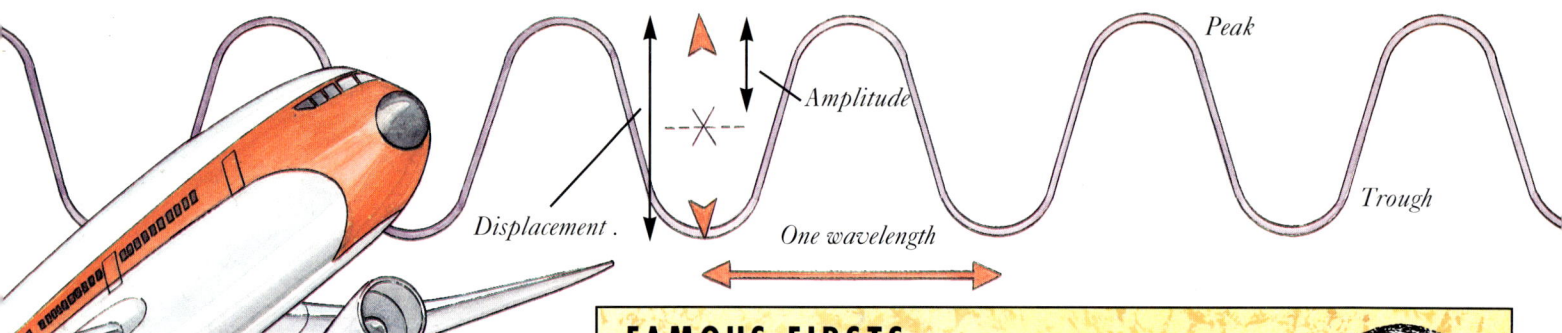

Peak

Amplitude

Displacement

One wavelength

Trough

Any sound, from a whisper to the deafening roar of a jet engine, can be represented as a wavy line, termed a sound wave, as shown above.

'waves'. These are usually drawn as a wavy line, like ripples on a pond. This idea of waves is useful for describing features of sound, such as wavelength and frequency. The wavelength is the distance between two similar points of successive waves. The frequency is the number of vibrations per second. It is related to a sound's pitch. Short wavelength and high frequency mean high pitch, such as a squeak. Long wavelength and low frequency mean low or deep pitch, such as a rumble.

In reality sound exists as the vibrations or movements of molecules. In air, the molecules are those of the various gases in the mixture, such as nitrogen and oxygen. A sound is the vibration of molecules in a certain way – a lot, then a little, then a lot again, and so on. As the molecules vibrate, they can

Gas molecules floating in air collide with each other and bounce away, in the same way that fast-moving marbles on a table rebound off each other.

FAMOUS FIRSTS

FREQUENCY AND WAVELENGTH

The wavelength is the distance between a point on one wave, such as the peak, and the same point on the next wave. It is usually measured in metres. The frequency is the number of complete waves passing a place in a certain time, usually one second. It is the same as the number of waves, vibrations or cycles per second. Frequency is measured in units called Hertz (Hz), named after German scientist Heinrich Hertz. The sound of the note middle C has a wavelength of 1.2 metres and a frequency of 256 Hertz. As the wavelength gets longer, the frequency gets lower and the sound is deeper in pitch. Shorter wavelengths mean higher frequencies and sounds which are shriller in pitch.

Heinrich Hertz (1857–1894)

SPECIAL FX

WHEN SOUNDS TRAVEL FASTER

Sound vibrations travel not only through air, but also through other gases, liquids and solids. In fact sounds travel much faster, and farther, through most liquids and solids, compared to air (see page 17). This includes the solid ground below our feet. So if you put your ear to the ground you may hear the drumming of an approaching vehicle, or the thud of steps, before these sounds reach you through the air. This is why expert trackers and scouts lie down and listen to the ground – to detect the thud of distant hoofs or the rumble of faraway wheels.

The thunderous hooves of migrating wildebeest can be heard sooner and more clearly from several kilometres away by listening through the ground rather than the air.

BOUNCING SOUNDS

When sound waves in air reach a solid what happens next depends on the nature of the substance. If it is hard and smooth, like stiff card or a brick wall, the sounds bounce off in the same way that light rays bounce back from a mirror. We call this reflection. The reflected sound is known as an echo. If the solid substance is uneven and soft, like cotton wool, it absorbs much of the sound energy. So there is little or no reflection. This test shows that sounds reflect from a surface at the same angle at which they hit it.

You need

Piece of thick, stiff card, sound source such as a ticking clock, two tubes of card about 40 centimetres long and 5-10 centimetres wide.

1. Prop the card vertically so that it is held firmly. Place a tube at an angle just in front of it. Put the clock at the other end of the tube. Sound waves travel along the tube, hit the card and reflect or bounce off.

2. Put one end of the other tube near the card, to catch the echoes. Listen at the tube's other end and alter its angle until the echoes are loudest. This should be at an equal but opposite angle to the first tube. Repeat the test after altering the angle of the first tube, to check your results.

FASCINATING FACTS

- Modern reptiles make few sounds. Dinosaurs could have been mainly silent too, unlike those in films.

- Sounds can travel and be heard under water. But it is difficult to talk with a breathing tube in your mouth. So divers use visible hand signals instead of communicating by speech or other sounds.

Okay

Yes

No

- There is no air or anything else in deep space. So sounds cannot travel through it. In real life, spacecraft would be totally silent.

Sound produced
[by voice-box]

- **Human**   80–1,500 Hz
- **Cat**   750–1,500 Hz
- **Robin**   2,000–15,000 Hz
- **Bat**   10,000–150,000 Hz
- **Dolphin**   200–200,000 Hz

Sound detected
[by ears]

- **Human**   25–20,000 Hz
- **Cat**   60–60,000 Hz
- **Robin**   250–20,000 Hz
- **Bat**   1,000–200,000 Hz
- **Dolphin**   150–200,000 Hz

The sounds produced by different devices and animals vary widely across the frequency spectrum, from extremely low-pitched to incredibly high. We can only hear some of them because our ears detect a limited range of frequencies.

be squeezed closer together (compressed), or spaced farther apart (expanded). In air, these are regions of high and low air pressure. The regions pass outward from the sound source, like ripples on a pond. The water molecules in the pond's ripple bob up and down, but otherwise they do not move far. Air molecules do much the same as a sound passes through air. Even with an extremely loud sound, air molecules vibrate by only 0.1 millimetres.

FAMOUS FIRSTS

TRUMPETERS ON A TRAIN
Austrian physicist Christian Doppler (1803–1853) discovered the effect named after him in 1842 (see below). At the time, there were few ways of travelling fast enough for people to hear it clearly. In 1845 the effect was demonstrated by a group of trumpet players, who rode in a railway carriage at high speed past the listeners.

The Doppler effect happens with light from stars. If a star is moving away from us, its individual light pattern is moved or shifted towards the red end of the light spectrum. Astronomers use this 'red shift' to calculate distances and speeds of stars.

SPECIAL FX

THE DOPPLER EFFECT
Listen to a car next time one speeds past. The sound from its engine seems to change from higher to lower. This is the Doppler effect. Any source producing sound and moving along, goes a short distance between sending out each wave. So the waves travelling forward from it are 'squeezed' closer together, while those behind are 'stretched' farther apart. Closer waves mean a higher frequency or pitch, which you hear as the sound-maker approaches you. When it passes you hear waves which are farther apart, with a lower frequency or pitch.

Moving sound source

Sound waves farther apart [lower frequency and pitch].

Sound waves closer together [higher frequency and pitch].

We can hear some of the clicks and squeaks made by dolphins. They also make other sounds too high for our ears, which other dolphins can hear.

NEEEE-AAAA-OOOOW

The faster a sound source moves, and the purer the sound it makes, then the clearer you can hear the Doppler effect. It happens well with the engines in motorcycles, which run very fast with a high-pitched whine. But you can test the Doppler effect even at low speeds, if you use a sound source with a pure and fairly high frequency, like a whistle.

You need

Friend with a bicycle, whistle, an open and safe place to cycle relatively fast.

1. Stand or sit still in the middle of the space. Your friend begins to cycle towards you from one end, speeding up to as fast as safely possible.

2. As your friend gets to within about 10 metres of you, they blow the whistle, and continue to blow while going past, to about 10 metres on the other side.

3. You should hear the whistle suddenly fall in pitch slightly, from higher to lower, as your friend goes past. This is the Doppler effect. Listen to the whistle while you are both still. Its pitch should be somewhere in the middle.

- The Doppler effect is most noticeable when listening to racing cars, vehicles sounding a siren, and jet planes.

- The Doppler effect applies to any type of wave, where the wave source is moving relative to the receiver. This includes sound and electromagnetic waves such as radio, microwaves, visible light and X-rays.

- The speed-measuring radar devices, or 'radar traps', used by police rely on the Doppler effect. So do some types of satellite navigation used by aircraft, ships, map-makers, surveyors and explorers.

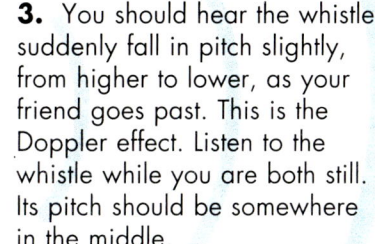

NATURAL SOUNDS

I t is a rural summer's day. Birds twitter, a cow chews the cud, and a slight breath of breeze stirs the leaves. But wait. There is a peal of thunder. The birds squawk and the cows grunt, as the wind whips through the branches. Natural sounds have many sources and meanings.

Snow falls and settles in virtual silence. But when many tonnes of snow slide in an avalanche, it crackles, grates and scrapes, and makes the ground tremble.

Anywhere on Earth, you can hear the sounds of nature. They come mainly from natural events, from the weather and from living things. Natural events vary from the deafening roar of a volcanic eruption to a shuddering clap of thunder, from the scrabbling and sliding of a rockfall to the eerie whooshing and crunching of a snow avalanche, and from the thunderous booming of a water-fall to the sharp cracks and hisses of a bushfire. The weather gives us many familiar daily sounds, which vary from comforting to nerve-jangling and can affect our moods and emotions. Wind blows gently or howls angrily. Rain patters lightly on window panes, or splatters fiercely. Waves lap quietly on sandy beaches, then crash with ferocious power against the rocks. A tinkling stream may swell into a raging torrent. All these sounds come from movements and vibrations of objects, which produce sound waves in the surrounding air.

There are also hundreds of natural voices – the sounds that creatures make as they go about their daily lives. Some are gentle and soothing to our ears, such as the cooing of pigeons and the purring of cats. Others are harsh

FAMOUS FIRSTS

Sound pulses reflect from objects, including prey

Flying bat emits high-frequency sound pulses

Bat hears sound echoes

NAVIGATING BY SOUND
Bats find their way in the dark by using their ears. A flying bat emits high-frequency squeaks and clicks, mostly too shrill for our ears but not for the bat. The sounds bounce off close objects. The bat listens to the pattern of returning echoes and works out the size and shape of items around it. The system is called echolocation and is a type of sonar (see page 43). It was first studied in bats by Donald Griffin in the late 1930s, at Harvard University in the USA. He was following earlier research by Italian scientist Lazarro Spallanzani (see opposite).

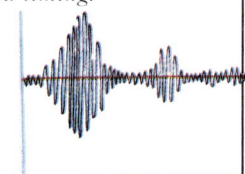

Sonagrams are diagrams of sounds, showing their frequency and timing.

This one shows two of a bat's echolocation clicks.

DIY SCIENCE

THE DAWN CHORUS
At dawn birds sing to tell each other who lives where, who is looking for a mate and who is in charge of a territory. Note the calls of various birds and write them in a nature diary. Does the dawn chorus begin at the same time each day, or is it linked to the sun rising? Do the species sing in the same order each morning?

WIND WHISTLES AND HOWLS

How does the wind make so many different noises as it blows among trees or buildings? The moving air sets up vibrations as it goes through gaps or openings. These vibrations create sound waves. You can see this with a wind-tube. You do not need a breeze. Simply hold one end of the tube and whirl the other end around, so that it passes through the air (rather than the air blowing past it) to give a wind effect.

You need

A tube of flexible plastic about 1 metre long and 5-10 centimetres wide, paper funnel, plastic sheet, sticking tape, scissors.

1. Swirl the tube around so that 'wind' passes the moving end. Hear how it hums or howls, like wind blowing past a small opening. Does your speed of whirling affect the pitch or loudness?

2. Enlarge the size of the opening at the whirling end by taping a funnel to it Does this alter the sound produced in pitch or loudness?

3. Make the opening smaller by covering the end with plastic sheet, with a small hole carefully cut in it. How does it sound now? What happens if you whirl the tube outside in a real wind?

- Lazarro Spallanzani was the first scientist to think that bats did not need their eyes to fly in the dark. In the 1790s he tested pipistrelle bats in dark rooms to show they did not need sight to avoid obstacles. But if their ears were blocked, they flew less skillfully. He proposed that bats could 'see with their ears'. People did not believe him, until scientists experimented with sound recorders, microphones and loudspeakers, over 100 years later.

- In the 1950s, American engineers set up a series of underwater 'listening posts' using microphones, to detect the sounds of enemy ships and sub-marines. The microphones picked up a deep humming noise with a constant frequency which could last for more than 30 minutes. The engineers were sure it was made by secret machinery, but it was the song made by the fin whale.

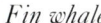
Drum fish

- Many animals are named after the sounds they make, such as the drum fish of seas and lakes, the bell-bird of Australia and the spring peeper frog of North America.

Fin whale

Many whales produce their songs in the 'sofar' layer, which is about 20–50 metres below the surface. Sounds travel well in water at this temperature and pressure.

and worrying, like a dog's snarl and a rabbit's squeal. Animals make these sounds for good reason. If we can learn the meanings of their songs and calls we can understand more about nature.

The lowest sounds in the African bush are the rumblings of the elephant, too deep for human ears. These sounds travel for several kilometres. The loudest sounds in the tropical jungle are the whoops of the howler monkey from South America.

DIY SCIENCE

HOWL LIKE THE HOWLER!
The howler monkey makes its incredibly loud call by blowing air through its enlarged voice-box and making this vibrate very strongly as a resonating chamber (see page 30).

You need
Several plastic drinks bottles, scissors.

1. Carefully cut one bottle halfway along. Place it near your mouth (never over the mouth) and whoop or howl loudly into it.

2. Alter the pitch and volume of your call, until you hear the bottle 'catch' the sound and make it louder, or amplify it. The bottle is acting like the howler monkey's huge voice-box – as a resonating chamber.

3. Cut other bottles to make chambers of various sizes. Which one resonates at the highest pitch?

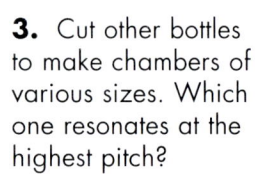

FASCINATING FACTS

THE CRICKET COMB
Crickets make chirps by rubbing a leg across a wing strut or vein. This has small 'teeth' along it. These catch on the vein or strut and produce sound waves. You can mimic a cricket using an ordinary plastic comb.

You need
Variety of large and small hair combs, materials such as card, plastic and metal.

FAMOUS FIRSTS

• Scientists continually discover new sounds in nature. For centuries crocodiles were believed to be terrible parents, sometimes even eating their babies. Now we know that the mother crocodile does not eat her young, but carries them to safety. When the babies are ready to hatch from their eggs in the riverbank soil, they squeak piercingly. The mother stands by to help them out of the shells. Then she ferries them in the safety of her mouth, down to the water.

Eating their young would not be a good survival strategy for crocodiles. In fact research shows that they are more intelligent creatures than lizards and snakes.

FASCINATING FACTS

Mynah

Macaw or parrot

• The world's loudest animal sounds are the deep grunts made by the world's largest animal, the blue whale. These grunts are estimated at 188 dB (see page 30) which would deafen a human. The grunts can be detected over a distance of 800 kilometres. Sounds travel more than four times faster in water, over 5000 kph (3100 mph), compared to air – and in steel, sound travels more than three times faster than in water.

• Some birds can imitate or copy various sounds, including other birds and animals, human voices, and even machines and engines. The Australian lyrebird can mimic a tractor, a chainsaw and a falling tree. Parrots and macaws are also fine mimics. There is no evidence however that such birds understand what they are saying.

Grasshoppers and crickets even when they are young also use their legs to leap between plants.

1. Hold the backbone of the comb firmly in one hand. Try not to touch the teeth, or they will not vibrate freely.

2. Scrape a material along the teeth so that they bend and spring back. Try moving it fast, then slowly. Does the pitch of the sound produced change?

3. Try out other combs. Do combs with long or short teeth give the highest note? Which type of objects give the loudest sounds?

MAKING SOUNDS

People have made sounds from the earliest times, from prehistoric grunts and yells to the millions of words in the 2000 or so languages of the modern world. Mammals and birds make sounds in a similar way to humans, using the voice-box in their necks. We have also invented sound-producing devices down the ages from ancient, simple musical instruments such as drums and pipes to today's hi-fi loudspeakers and headphones.

FAMOUS FIRSTS

THE ARMONICA
People have invented many musical instruments over the years, but not all have been successful. In the 1760s American scientist and statesman Benjamin Franklin devised the armonica. Its different-sized glass bowls revolved on a central spindle. Touch the rim of each bowl and it made a delicate humming note (like the wine glasses see page 21). Beethoven and Mozart wrote music for the armonica, but it was very difficult to tune and transport. It gradually fell from favour.

Benjamin Franklin (1706–1790) is well known for his experiments with static electricity.

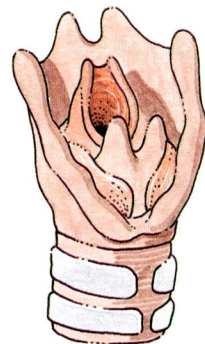

Vocal cords

Vocal cords pulled together and stretched to vibrate and make sounds.

Vocal cords apart for normal breathing.

This cut-away view of the head and neck shows the voice-box (or larynx) in position, plus two close-up views of the voice-box, in normal breathing and making sounds.

People with hearing problems may not hear their own voices, which can make it hard to learn to speak. It can help to feel the voice-box vibrations from another person, then feel their own voice-box to copy the vibrations by making the same sounds.

The most familiar sound of all is the human voice. It comes from the voice-box or larynx in the neck. This hollow chamber, at the base of the throat and top of the windpipe, has two pearl-white folds that stick out from its sides. They are the vocal folds, usually called the vocal cords. But they are shelf-like folds and vibrate along their free edge, rather than being string-like cords, which are free to vibrate along their lengths.

In normal breathing, the vocal cords are held apart by muscles of the larynx. To speak, the mus-cles pull the cords near each

SPECIAL FX

FEEL YOUR VOICE
Your vocal cords vibrate to make sounds, which emerge from your mouth and nose as sound waves. If these hit a flexible surface, they pass on their vibrations to it. This experiment uses a balloon as the flexible surface.

You need
A balloon, a friend.

1. Blow up the balloon quite large, but not too hard. Hold it lightly between your fingertips, 5 centimetres in front of your mouth. Your friend lightly touches its other side with fingertips.

2. Hum, talk or make some other loud noise. Your sound waves hit the balloon's side and make it vibrate. The vibrations pass through the rubbery skin, and both you and your friend should feel them.

FUNNY CORDS, FUNNY VOICES

There are many methods of copying the way that your own voice works, with two strips of flexible material close together and vibrating in a stream of air. Here are a few of them. Can you think of others?

You need
Balloon, long blade of grass, whoopee cushion, plastic hair comb and tracing or greaseproof paper.

1. Hold the long, flat blade of grass between your thumbs as shown. Put your thumbs to your lips and blow through.

Small air gap along each side of blade.

2. The grass should vibrate with a buzz or hum. Try arching your thumbs slightly more or less, to change the air gap and stretch or loosen the blade, for better results.

3. Fold a piece of tracing paper in half. Place the teeth of the comb in the fold.

4. Press your lips gently on to the paper and hum or blow. The paper vibrates between your lips and the comb teeth below. Vary the pitch of your hum, so you can play a tune.

Can you get a sound by folding the paper over the comb's backbone?

Stretch the neck wider or let it go looser. The pitch of the squeal should change, again like your vocal cords.

5. Blow up the balloon. Hold the neck firmly between thumb and fingers of each hand.

6. Let air out slowly. You should hear a squealing sound as the two sides of the neck vibrate. They work like your vocal cords, and the balloon is like your lungs, pushing air passed them.

7. Gently inflate the whoopee cushion. Then press or sit on it to expel the air.

8. Hear – and see – how the neck vibrates floppily to produce a familiar sound. The vibrations are much slower than those of the balloon neck, and so the pitch of the sound is far lower.

Vibrations may be slow enough to hear and see separately.

- The symbol for HMV or 'His Master's Voice', from RCA Victor (Record Company of America), shows a dog listening to an old-style gramophone playing a flat vinyl-type disc. The original painting *His Master's Voice* was by Francis Barraud in 1900, from a true scene. The dog's owner had made a recording of his voice on a disc. After he died, the dog would sit and listen attentively to his master's voice coming from the trumpet-shaped sound horn of the gramophone.

- The loudest natural sounds ever made on Earth are probably gigantic volcanic eruptions, such as the explosion of the island of Krakatoa (see page 24).

- Some of the loudest sounds produced by our own inventions are the noise of space rockets blasting from the launch pad. The biggest were the *Saturn V* rockets that launched the USA's Apollo moon missions of 1968–72. They had their greatest success when *Apollo 11* landed on the Moon – an airless and therefore completely silent place – on 20 July 1969. Once a space rocket has taken off and enters the vacuum of space, it becomes totally silent.

Radio sets began to appear in many homes in the 1920s. The loudspeaker was large and heavy. It was often muffled and dull-sounding compared to today's versions.

other and stretch them slightly. Air flows up from the lungs, through the thin gap between the cords, and makes them vibrate rapidly to and fro. These vibrations shake the air around them, setting up sound waves that travel with the air, up and out through the mouth. The sounds from the vocal cords themselves are quiet and lack feature. They are given extra volume and character by the throat, the insides of the mouth and nose, and the air-filled chambers called sinuses inside the skull bones. This is what makes your own voice unique among thousands of others. The sounds are shaped into words and other recognizable utterances by the movements of the jaws and teeth, cheeks, tongue and lips. To make higher notes, muscles in the larynx pull the cords longer and tighter, so that they vibrate at higher frequencies.

Most musical instruments work in a similar way. The vibrating string of a piano or guitar, or the vibrating body and the air inside a trumpet or tuba, produce sound waves. These travel outwards in all directions through the air, until they are absorbed, reflected or dampened.

Human voices and musical instruments are mechanical sound-makers. They produce

SPECIAL FX

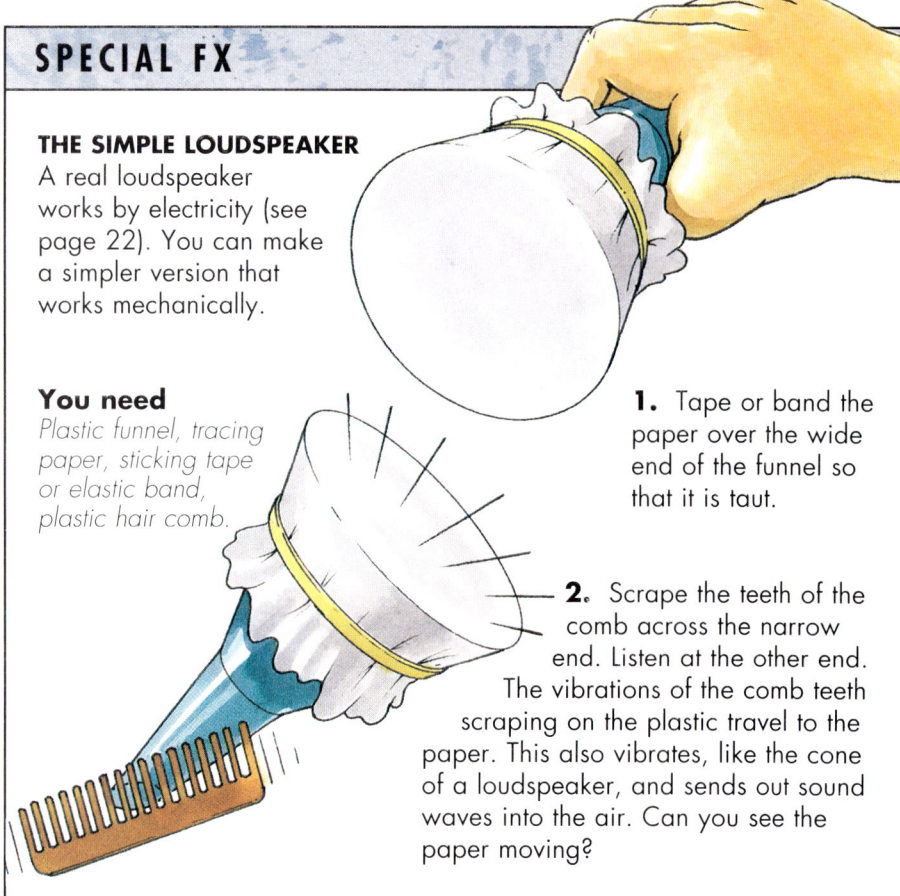

THE SIMPLE LOUDSPEAKER
A real loudspeaker works by electricity (see page 22). You can make a simpler version that works mechanically.

You need
Plastic funnel, tracing paper, sticking tape or elastic band, plastic hair comb.

1. Tape or band the paper over the wide end of the funnel so that it is taut.

2. Scrape the teeth of the comb across the narrow end. Listen at the other end. The vibrations of the comb teeth scraping on the plastic travel to the paper. This also vibrates, like the cone of a loudspeaker, and sends out sound waves into the air. Can you see the paper moving?

DIY SCIENCE

RINGING THE BELL
The electric bell uses the effects of magnetism and a make-and-break switch to make the clapper hit the tin-can 'bell' very fast, producing the ringing sound. This project requires an adult to do the drilling, cutting and screwing.

You need
Wooden baseboard, blocks of wood, insulated electrical wire, strips of iron or steel metal, large and small steel bolts with nuts, tin can, battery (4.5, 6 or 9 volts), glue, woodscrews, switch, an adult.

Read the instructions first, to see how the bell is made and works.

1. Drill a hole in one wood block for the large bolt. Glue and screw the blocks in position on the baseboard. Push the bolt through the hole.

2. Wind some wire around the bolt in a coil. This will work as an electromagnet and turn the bolt into a magnet when electricity flows.

3. Drill, bend and screw the two strips of metal to the middle block. The shorter is a make-and-break switch. The longer strip is the bell clapper, which should be near the end of the large bolt, but not touching it.

4. Glue the small nut to the block top. Screw the bolt into it, so it just touches the shorter metal strip. Glue or screw the tin can near the clapper end.

PLAY A DELICATE TUNE

Wine-glasses are delicate. They may crack or break, with the risk of cuts, so get an adult to do this.

You need
Eight wine-glasses, water, safe and flat tabletop, an adult.

1. Place the glasses in a row. Put a little water into one. Hold its base with one hand. Dip a fingertip of the other hand in the water and stroke it gently around the rim.

2. Alter the speed and pressure of the rubbing. The glass bowl should vibrate to produce an eerie, delicate humming sound.

Hold the base, not the bowl, or this will reduce its vibrations.

3. Put increasing amounts of water in the glasses. Alter these so that the glasses play the notes of a musical scale when rubbed (page 45). Now you can practise playing tunes.

- Thin-glass goblets can vibrate when hit by sound waves. This is due to resonance (see page 32). Some singers listen to the note produced when a glass is tapped and then sing the same note back at the glass, so that their voice vibrates the glass so much that it shatters.

- The same may happen to glass windows when vibrated by sound waves. In one church, the loud clang of a large bell shattered the stained-glass window above the altar.

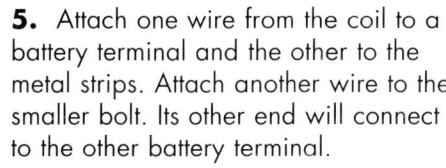

5. Attach one wire from the coil to a battery terminal and the other to the metal strips. Attach another wire to the smaller bolt. Its other end will connect to the other battery terminal.

Bend the clapper so it hits the bell clearly.

6. Join this wire to the battery. Electricity flows in a circuit. The large bolt becomes a magnet and attracts the metal strips. They pull across, clang the bell and break the circuit at the smaller bolt. The magnetism switches off. The metal strips spring back and remake the circuit. The cycle repeats to give a ringing sound.

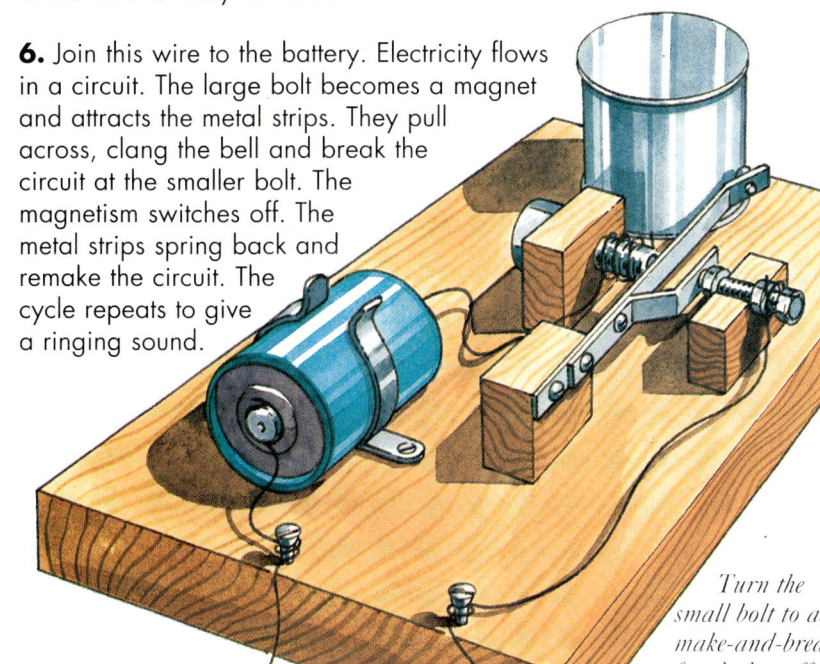

Turn the small bolt to adjust the make-and-break switch for the best effect.

In a modern rock concert, the human voice would be too weak to hear by itself. It is made louder by electrical amplification.

sound waves from kinetic energy, the energy of motion. Sound is also a form of energy, so the kinetic energy is transformed or converted into sound energy. However sound is a fairly weak type of energy compared to heat, electricity and other forms. If you could collect all the energy in the cheering and clapping sounds made by a huge crowd at a sports event, it would be hardly enough heat to boil a kettle of water.

Today we have other ways of making sounds. The main one is the loudspeaker, used in tape players, television sets, hi-fis and other kinds of audio equipment, as the final link to turn electricity into sound. It uses the principle of electromagnetism. A varying pattern of electricity passes through a wire coil. This turns the coil into an electromagnet, whose magnetism interferes with a nearby permanent (ordinary) magnet. The two magnets alternatively attract and repel each other, making the coil move, or vibrate. It is attached to a cone shape of card or plastic, and so

The loudspeaker's cone is attached to a coil of wire, around or inside a strong magnet. Varying amounts of electricity flow through the wire, representing the patterns of sound. This turns the coil into a varying electromagnet, which vibrates as it is moved by the permanent magnet. The moving coil makes the cone vibrate and send out sound waves.

FAMOUS FIRSTS

THE ORCHESTRAL SOUND-MAKERS
The musical instruments in the orchestra have changed over the years, as new ones have replaced older types. The origins of some instruments can be pinpointed to the date when they were invented. Others have gradually changed and modified from previous versions, over years and even centuries.

The basic trumpet shape was devised by the Ancient Egyptians over 3000 years ago. It was short and straight, with no valves (pressed keys). The tube became longer and looped around in an oval during the 15th century. The valves were added in the 1820s.

The clarinet has a vibrating strip, called a reed, in the mouthpiece. It was first made in about 1710 by Jacob Denner in Nuremberg, Germany, but did not become popular until about 1750.

In today's symphony orchestra each group of instruments has a standard position. This gives the best overall combination of sounds for the audience.

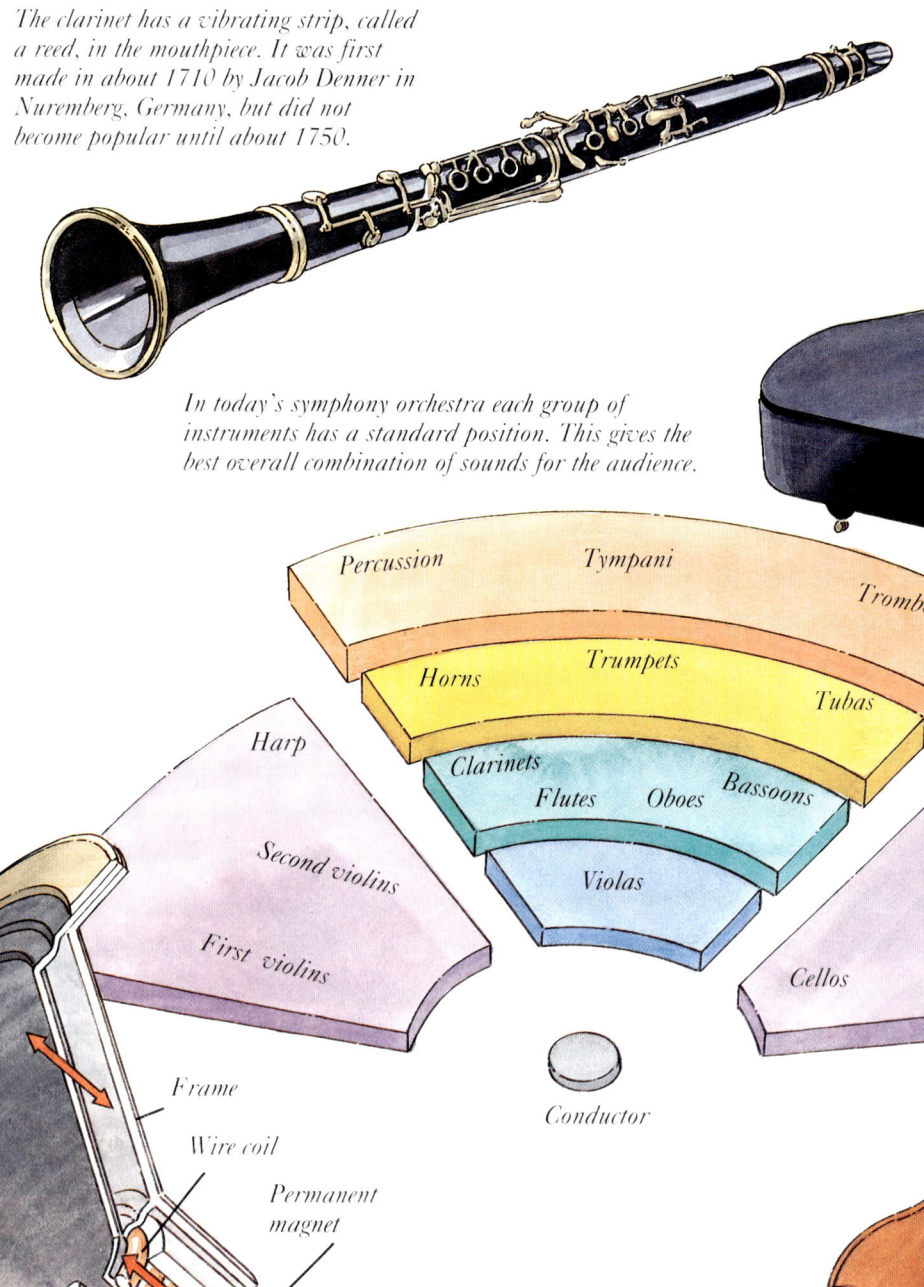

Percussion
Tympani
Trombo[
Horns
Trumpets
Tubas
Harp
Clarinets
Flutes
Oboes
Bassoons
Second violins
Violas
First violins
Cellos
Conductor

Loudspeaker box of body

Frame

Wire coil

Card or plastic cone

Permanent magnet

The earliest harps were plucked in Sumeria over 4000 years ago. This stringed instrument has been through many sizes and designs around the world. The modern harp was designed by Erard, the French company of piano- and harp- makers, in about 1810.

The piano's forerunner was the harpsichord, in which the strings are plucked. A piano's strings are hit by felt hammers. Its full name is pianoforte, and the first versions were made from 1698 by Bartolomeo Cristofori in Florence, Italy. The piano was then improved by stages in Germany, Austria, England and America.

The modern violin, with four strings, came into being in about 1510. It was developed from two similar medieval instruments, the fiddle and the rebec. The strings are vibrated by a bow.

DIY SCIENCE

THE TWANGING GUITAR
A vibrating string changes pitch with length.

You need
Ruler, pencils, rubber bands of various thicknesses.

1. Stretch the band over the ruler. Slide the pencils under the band at each end of the ruler, so the band's top part can vibrate freely. Pluck the band. Listen to its note. Slide the pencils closer, so the vibrating part of the band is shorter. Pluck again. Has the note changed?

2. Using the scale on the ruler, contrast the notes from a certain length of band (say, 26 centimetres) with the note from half this length (say, 13 centimetres). Does one note sound twice as high as the other? (See also page 33.)

3. Try other thicknesses of band and vary their tension. When the same length of band is twanged, does a thicker band make a different note to a thinner one?

FASCINATING FACTS

- Three original pianos built by the inventor Bartolomeo Cristofori still survive. The oldest, dated 1720, is in New York. The others are in Rome (1722) and Leipzig (1726).

- A few musical instruments are named after their inventors. From the 1840s came the saxophone, after Belgian instrument-maker Adolphe Sax. Another is the sousaphone of 1898, after the American marching-music composer John Philip Sousa. Much more modern is the moog electronic synthesizer (pronounced 'mowg'). The first version was made in 1964 by American electronics expert Robert Moog.

- Some musical instruments have developed from devices used originally to send sound signals for communication. Some of the best examples are drums and horns (see below).

- Some composers have written musical works for very strange instruments. There have been several 'junkyard' concertos, including sounds such as banging car doors, blaring car horns, thumping empty oil drums, clanking chains, the crunch of a car-crusher and the deep throb of a bulldozer's diesel engine.

- One musical piece has no sounds at all. It is called *4 minutes 33 seconds*. It was 'written' by the American composer John Cage in 1954. A pianist sits at the piano and plays nothing for exactly 4 minutes and 33 seconds.

- In the Alps mountains of Europe the long wooden trumpet called the alphorn was used by herdsmen to call each other. Also called the alpenhorn and alpine horn, its loud, deep trumpeting sound echoed across the valleys and summoned people to church – or to war. Similar instruments were used in upland regions of Germany, Scandinavia and Eastern Europe.

In 1883 a volcano erupted on the small island of Krakatoa, near Sumatra in South-East Asia. The island blew apart and disappeared, and the immense roar of the eruption was heard 3000 kilometres away. It was the loudest sound recorded by humans.

this vibrates too, and sends out sound waves into the air. Earphones use a similar but much smaller device, or one based on crystals which vibrate as the varying electricity goes through them.

Loudspeakers did not become available until the 1910s. They had to wait for the invention of the right piece of electrical equipment – the triode, or amplifying valve, by American Lee Forest in 1906. This boosted the electricity so that it was powerful enough to move the loudspeaker. Today sound can be produced first in electrical form, as in the electric guitar or synthesizer. Or sound waves can be changed into electricity by the microphone (see page 28). Most manipulation of sound, such as in a recording studio, is now done while it is patterns of electric currents. The loudspeaker then turns it back into sound waves.

FAMOUS FIRSTS

THROUGH THE SOUND BARRIER

The speed of sound in air varies with temperature and height, slowing to about 1062 kph (660 mph) at high altitudes. The first person to go faster than sound, was Charles Yeager. On 14 October 1947 he piloted the rocket-engined *Bell X-1* to 1078 kph (670 mph) at an altitude of 12,800 metres. People feared the plane would shake and fall to bits as it tried to 'break the sound barrier'.But all went smoothly and the 'sound barrier' was no barrier at all.

The orange Bell X-1, nicknamed 'Glamorous Glennis' after Yeager's wife, was launched from under a B-29 Superfortress bomber at a height of 3600 metres.

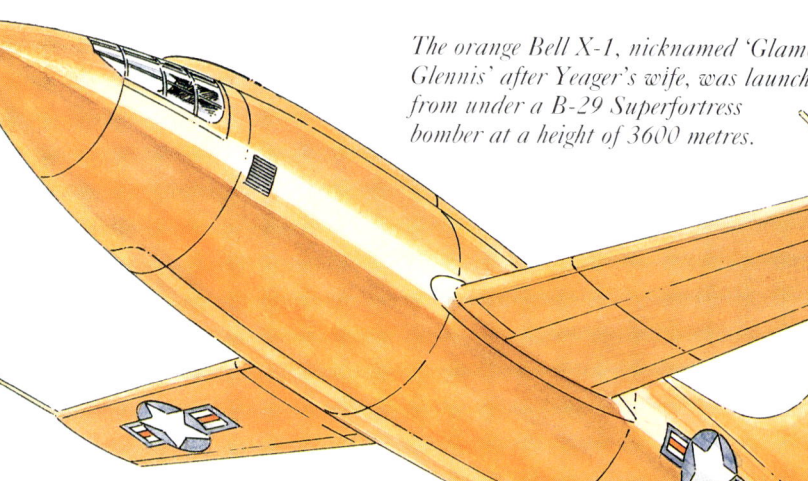

FAMOUS FIRSTS

ELECTRIC INSTRUMENTS

People used microphones, amplifiers and loudspeakers to pick up the sounds of instruments and make them louder. But the first popular instrument to be based on electricity, rather than make sound waves, was the electric guitar. The metal strings vibrate near the pick-up, a magnet with a coil of wire around it. The shaking string disturbs the magnetism, and this alters the electric current. The earliest electric guitars were made in the 1930s.

Fender Broadcaster, an early mass-produced electric guitar with a solid body (1950).

The keyboard of the electric organ produces electrical signals, not sounds. Loudspeakers turn the electricity into sound.

Magnetic pick-ups

SHOOTING WITH SOUND

You need
Card tube, sheets of thin card and thin plastic, pencil, sticking tape, rubber band, scissors.

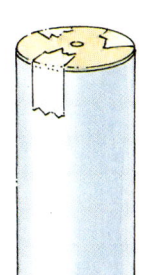

1. Draw around the end of the tube on to the card.

2. Cut out the resulting card disc.

3. Push the pencil point through the disc's centre to make a small hole.

4. Tape the disc firmly to one end of the tube, so the hole is central.

5. Place the plastic or tracing paper sheet over the other end and secure with the band, so the sheet is stretched tight.

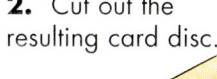

Flick the plastic hard to produce sharp, powerful sound waves.

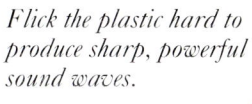

6. Cut a thin strip of card, fold at right angles and tape it down. This is the 'target'.

7. Point the sound gun at the target. Tap or flick the sheeted end hard. The target should move, battered by the concentrated blast of sound waves.

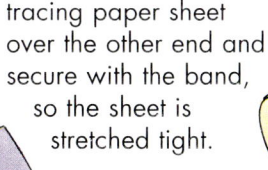

The waves are concentrated and travel down the tube.

The hole allows the sound waves to escape in a concentrated 'beam'.

SPECIAL FX

SOUND FX

When you listen to radio or television, or to a tape or disc, sounds may not be what they seem. Creaky doors, hitting hammers, howling wind and many other noises may be 'sound effects'. They are made separately and added in, or dubbed, later.

Chopping cabbage sounds like squashed flesh.

A large floppy sheet can be shaken to sound like thunder.

Empty shoes in a sand tray sound like someone walking on gravel.

Coconut shells clicked together sound like a horse's hoofs.

FASCINATING FACTS

- Middle C, with a frequency of 256 Hertz (see page 10), is near the top of the singing range of a typical adult male voice. It is also near the lower end of the singing range of an adult female voice.

- The average length of a man's vocal cords is 21 millimetres, compared to 17 millimetres for a woman.

- A boy's voice goes crackly and deepens during the teenage years. This is because hormonal changes in the body make the vocal cords thicker and stiffer, so they vibrate at lower frequencies.

The outer ear flap collects sound waves and funnels them towards the eardrum. This thin, flexible, skin-like membrane vibrates as sound waves hit it. The vibrations pass along a chain of three tiny bones, the ossicles, to the snail-shaped cochlea. Inside the cochlea the vibrations produce ripples in a fluid which are turned into electrical nerve signals.

DETECTING SOUNDS

The two sound receivers on either side of the human head are incredibly sensitive at detecting sound waves. They can adapt instantly from straining to hear a whisper to coping with a jet plane roaring overhead. But our ears have their limits. All around us is an 'ocean' of invisible sound – but we only hear some of it.

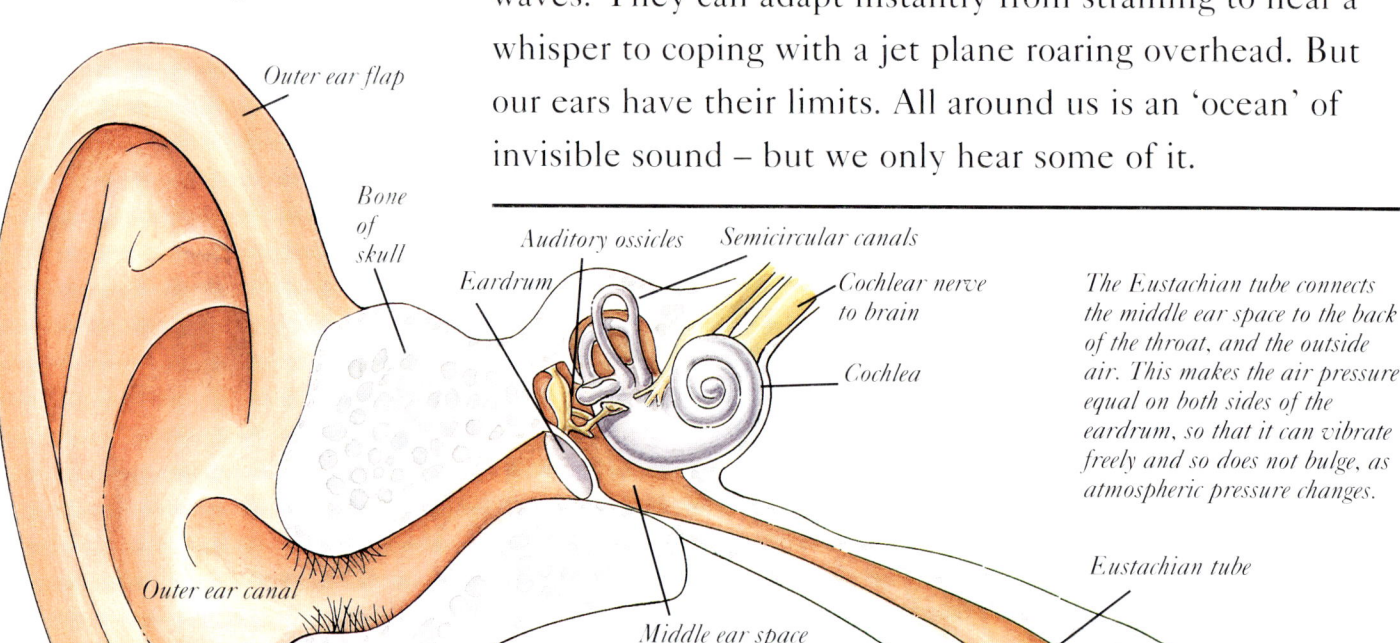

Outer ear flap

Bone of skull

Auditory ossicles   Semicircular canals

Eardrum

Cochlear nerve to brain

Cochlea

The Eustachian tube connects the middle ear space to the back of the throat, and the outside air. This makes the air pressure equal on both sides of the eardrum, so that it can vibrate freely and so does not bulge, as atmospheric pressure changes.

Eustachian tube

Outer ear canal

Middle ear space

Ear lobe

We tend to think that sounds we can hear are the only sounds that exist. But watch a dog or horse – their ears may prick up when we hear nothing. Human ears are very sensitive, but they cannot hear all the sounds that come through the air. Our ears have a limited ability to detect sounds.

A typical person can hear sounds from about 25 Hertz (Hz), vibrations or cycles per second, up to about 20,000 Hertz. Sounds with frequencies lower than 25 Hertz do not stimulate the ear, so we are unaware of them. Yet they do exist and some animals can

FASCINATING FACTS

- Some animals can hear ultra-sonic sounds which are too high for human ears. Dogs, dolphins and bats can hear frequencies of 200,000 Hertz or more.

A grasshopper's ears are on its knees.

Large outer ears pick up faint sounds.

A toad has an eardrum on either side of its head, behind the eye, showing as a disc of 'skin'.

Most birds have ears under their feathers.

Fish detect vibrations using the silvery lateral line along the middle of the body.

HOW THE EAR HEARS

This model ear works in a similar way to the real human ear, but you can see the results.

You need

Thick and thin card, plastic 'bendy' drinking straw, table-tennis ball, side part of baking tin, clingfilm, glue, sticking tape, bowl of water, pencil, scissors, adult supervision.

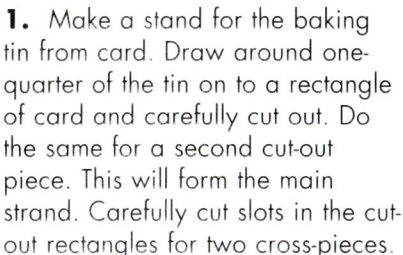

1. Make a stand for the baking tin from card. Draw around one-quarter of the tin on to a rectangle of card and carefully cut out. Do the same for a second cut-out piece. This will form the main strand. Carefully cut slots in the cut-out rectangles for two cross-pieces.

Glue flaps together

2. Tape or glue the cross-pieces in place as shown to make the stand.

3. Stretch the clingfilm over the tin so that it is taut with no creases or tears. Tape the film in place, taking care not to poke or stretch it. This is the 'eardrum'.

4. Carefully cut and bend a sheet of thin card to make a double-folded triangle. Fold back the two long edges and glue them so that the card triangle is open on one side only.

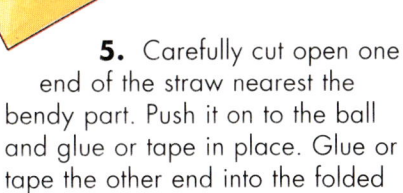

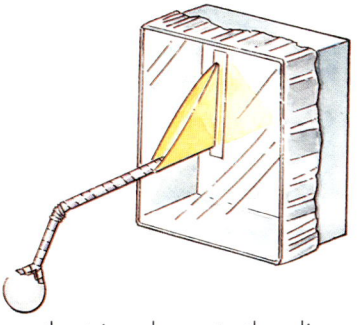

5. Carefully cut open one end of the straw nearest the bendy part. Push it on to the ball and glue or tape in place. Glue or tape the other end into the folded card triangle.

6. Tape the triangle on to the clingfilm with card strips, with the straw at the centre. The straw acts like a lever to enlarge vibrations in the same way as the ossicle bones in the real ear.

Try sounds of different volume and pitch. Do they produce different types of ripple?

7. Place the tin on the stand near the bowl. Adjust the straw so the ball just dips in the water. Shout at the 'eardrum'. Sound waves hit it and make it vibrate, which causes the ball to vibrate too. This produce ripples in the water, like the ripples in the fluid of the ear's cochlea. This is how you see the sounds.

DIRECTION OF SOUND

Sounds from one side appear louder in one ear than in the other. As sound waves travel quite slowly, they reach the nearer ear before the farther one. The brain works out volume and time differences, to tell a sound's source. Make sounds from various positions for a blindfolded friend to guess their direction.

detect them. Also sounds above 20,000 Hertz do not affect our ears, although they may be heard by other animals. Sounds too low for our hearing range are known as infrasound, whilst those which are too high are called ultrasound.

Ears detect sounds, but do not process them. The ear converts the energy of sound waves into the energy of patterns of tiny electrical signals called nerve impulses. These go along nerves to the brain and reach the parts called the auditory centres. Here the patterns of nerve impulses are sorted and processed, compared with information in the brain's memory, and passed to the conscious, thinking centres of the brain. The result is you become aware of the sounds and are able to identify them – or not!

A microphone works in a similar way to an ear. It also converts patterns of sound waves

The moving-coil microphone has a diaphragm membrane, like an eardrum, which vibrates from sound waves. This makes a coil of wire move in a magnetic field, which alters the pattern of electricity flowing through the wire.

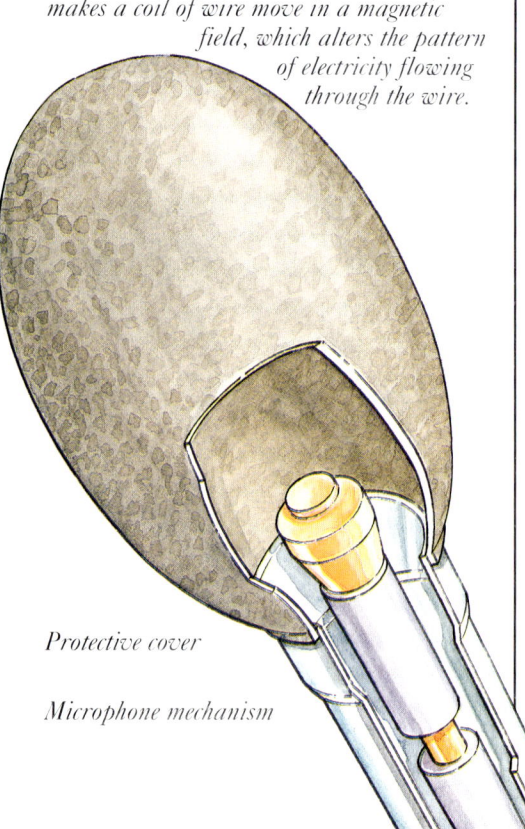

Protective cover

Microphone mechanism

TALKING BY TELEPHONE

From the 1840s people could communicate across long distances by sending electrical signals along wires by telegraph. Scottish-born American scientist Alexander Graham Bell (1847–1922) wanted to send signals which represented the sounds of speech, rather than the dot-dash system of Morse code. He finally succeeded in 1876 with his 'speaking telegraph'. It used the electromagnetic effect similarly to the modern microphone. A flexible sheet or diaphragm was attached to a coil of wire and made it vibrate in a magnetic field, creating a pattern of electric current that copied the pattern of sound waves. The transmitter (mouthpiece) and receiver (earpiece) of Bell's first telephone were almost the same, but worked in opposite ways.

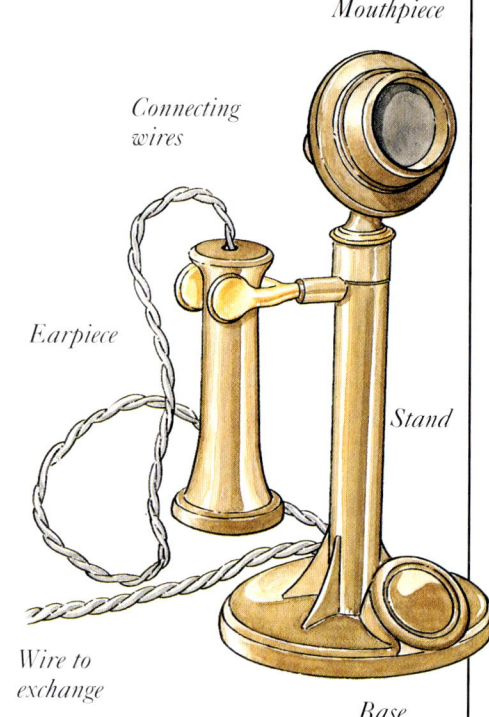

Mouthpiece

Connecting wires

Earpiece

Stand

Wire to exchange

Base

A common telephone design of about 1910.

THE EAR OF THE TELEPHONE

Once Bell had produced his early telephones, the great American inventor Thomas Edison (1847–1931) devised his own version. This differed in the mouthpiece, which is the 'microphone' of the telephone. Edison's version had a small container or capsule of tiny grains of carbon. Electricity passed though it. Sound waves hit a diaphragm, attached to the capsule, and squashed or stretched the grains. This altered the amount of electricity passing through in a pattern that represented the sound waves. Edison's carbon-button basic design is still used in many telephones today.

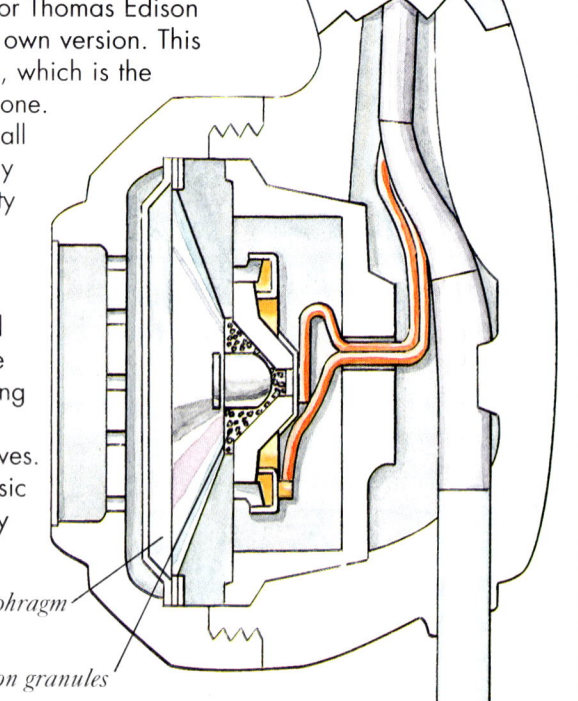

Diaphragm

Carbon granules

DIY SCIENCE

STRINGING WORDS TOGETHER

The vibrations of sound pass through liquids and solids, as well as the gases in air. Study this with the can-and-string telephone.

You need

Selection of cup-shaped items, such as thin plastic cup, thick plastic cup, heat-insulating ('polystyrene') cup and cardboard toilet roll, selection of strings and threads such as cotton, woollen yarn, natural string, plastic twine and fishing line, scissors, friend, adult supervision.

1. You can also make your own cups by stretching clingfilm or tracing paper over a cardboard roll and taping it in place. Try the same with a wooden tube too.

Making a cup out of a cardboard tube.

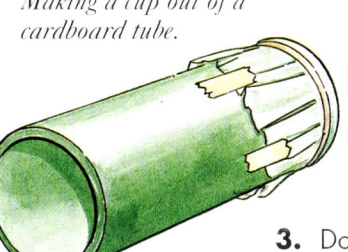

2. Begin with thin plastic cups and parcel string. With the scissors point, make a tiny hole in the base of each cup. Poke the string through this and tie a large retaining knot. Or tie the string around a paper clip and pull this flat on to the cup's base.

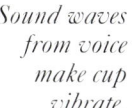

3. Do the same at the other end, leaving about 3 metres of string between the cups.

4. You and a friend each hold a cup by its rim. Let the string flop and coil on to the ground. Speak into the cup while your friend listens into the other cup.

5. Now pull the string taut and repeat step 4. Does the telephone work best with a loose or taut string?

Making hole in base of cup

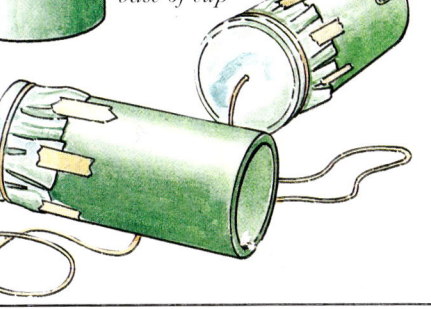

Sound waves from voice make cup vibrate.

6. Your friend then speaks into her or his cup, while you listen into yours. It helps if you say 'Over' each time you have finished and you expect a reply. What happens if you both speak at once?

7. Make different versions of the telephone using different cups and strings. Which work best? Are the results improved when you pull the string as tight as possible?

FASCINATING FACTS

- Stage performers sometimes use a microphone on a stand, which hears their voices and instruments and feeds the electrical signals into the main amplification or PA (public address) system. The sounds can also be picked up by microphones along the front of the stage.

- At a large performance there may over 100 microphones for performers, instruments, sound effects and even audience noise. The signals from them are combined at a large mixing desk operated by the sound engineers.

At important press events, each radio station, television channel and newspaper team used to have a large microphone to detect the speaker's voice. Today, they usually agree to share a few small microphones.

into corresponding patterns of electrical signals. These go along a wire to an amplifier, which makes the signals stronger. The electrical signals can be altered by various means, such as boosting low frequencies, and then fed into a loudspeaker or earphones so that they are turned back into sound waves.

Electrical amplification of sounds, to make them louder, is common today – from the battery-operated police loudhailer to the giant amplifiers and speakers at a disco club or musical performance. Such amplification depended on the invention of suitable electrical equipment, including triode valves (see page 24) in the 1900s. Before this time people had to rely on the natural loudness of their voices, musical instruments, bells and other sound producers.

A vital feature of acoustics is resonance. Each object has a natural frequency of vibration, from a human voice-box to a wooden board and from a guitar body to a bell. It depends on the object's size and shape, the thickness and flexibility of its material, how much air it encloses, and many other factors. When bashed or shaken the object vibrates at its natural resonant frequency and so produces sounds of a certain

A sound's intensity, similar to loudness or volume, is measured in bels, named after Alexander Graham Bell (see page 28). The bel is a very large unit, so the loudness scale is shown in decibels (dB, one-tenth of a bel). This chart shows some examples. Noises greater than 85 decibels can harm the ears.

HEAR AND BE HEARD!

The megaphone and the ear trumpet both work in the same way. They are not electrical, so they cannot increase the total volume of a sound. But they can collect and funnel the sound waves, concentrating them like a lens focuses a light beam. The sounds become louder where you want them, and quieter elsewhere.

You need

Large sheets of strong card, sticking tape, friend, tape measure, quiet place.

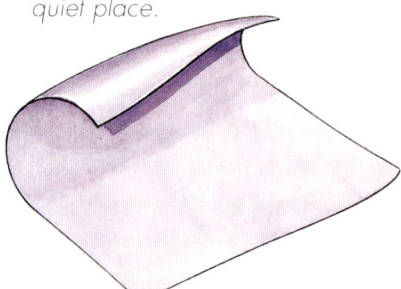

1. Roll the card into a funnel shape, with a 5-centimetre hole at the small end. Tape firmly. Repeat with the other card.

2. Stand 2 metres from your friend. Speak in your normal voice, reciting a phrase or saying. The friend walks away slowly, and signals where he or she can no longer hear you. Measure the distance between you both.

3. Repeat step 2, with your voice at the same volume and tone. But use the card funnel as if it were a megaphone, speaking through it so that the sound waves are beamed directly towards your friend. Is the distance greater?

4. Repeat step 2, without your megaphone, but your friend uses the card funnel as an ear trumpet.

5. Repeat a final time, you with the megaphone and your friend with the ear trumpet. Does this give the maximum distance?

0 dB Silence	*10 dB Distant leaves rustling*	*20 dB Watch ticking*	*30 dB Quiet bedroom at night*	*40 dB Quiet classroom at exam time*	*50 dB On the ban of a brook or stream*

SPECIAL FX

CHLADNI FIGURES

German scientist Ernst Chladni (1756–1827) experimented with the vibrations produced by sound waves. He scattered sand or sugar grains on very thin metal plates and vibrated the plates using a violin bow or sound waves. The grains took up intricate patterns on the plates, depending on which parts vibrated (according to the pitch and volume of the sound). The patterns are called Chladni figures. Modern versions of them are used to study the acoustic properties of musical instruments, loudspeakers, wall panels, windows and many other objects.

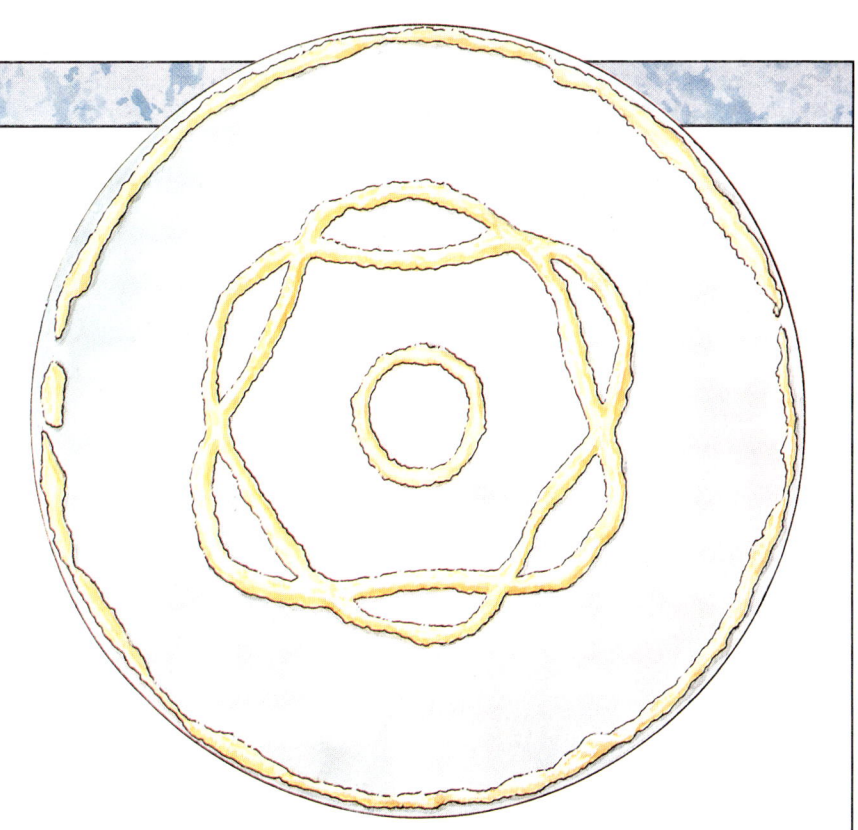

The sound waves of a human voice saying 'aah' make this thin, circular plate vibrate. The tiny, light grains on it take up a petal-like shape – one of many Chladni patterns.

FAMOUS FIRSTS

THE MYSTERY OF THE CRYSTAL

Crystals have many unusual properties. For example they allow electricity to pass through them but, if they are squeezed or stretched, they alter the amount of electricity. A crystal such as quartz that is squashed hard can generate electricity. The opposite also happens. By passing varying amounts of electricity through a crystal it changes its shape accordingly. This is the piezoelectric effect, discovered in 1880 by Pierre Curie (1859–1906) and his brother Jacques. It is used in various sound devices. For example a fast-changing electric current passed through a crystal makes it vibrate. If the crystal is attached to a diaphragm membrane, the vibrations produce sounds, especially ultrasound. The piezoelectric effect is also used in some microphones, headphones and vinyl record pick-ups.

Most high quality microphones are moving coil, not crystal

FASCINATING FACTS

- The first electrical hearing aid was devised in the USA by Millar Hutchinson in 1902.

- Ear trumpets used in Ancient Greece and Rome were crafted from metals and decorated with jewels.

dB People ...ng, about ...metre apart | *70 dB Hum of conversation in classroom* | *80 dB Cars on a main road, from the pavement* | *90 dB Underground train at speed* | *100 dB Very loud disco [exceeding legal noise limit]* | *110 dB Pneumatic hammer or road drill, if you were using it!* | *120 dB Jet engine only 10 metres away*

pitch. Objects such as musical instruments are designed and built to resonate well at certain frequencies. In effect this makes them sound louder and produce purer tones at particular pitches.

Resonance can pass from one object to another. This is sympathetic resonance. It can be used to advantage in designing concert halls and studios. But it creates problems too. In an orchestra when a musician plays a solo, the sound waves emitted can set up sympathetic resonance in other instruments, such as cellos and drums, causing an unwanted 'mumble' of sounds.

Many towns and cities are full of invisible pollution – noise. Continuous loud sounds of road vehicles, aeroplanes, trains, people, animals and machinery cause stress and various symptoms of illness, such as headaches. Some workers wear ear-defenders to protect their hearing. Noise meters measure the loudness in decibels.

DIY SCIENCE

THE GHOST GUITARIST
Resonance can be shown with two stringed instruments, such as piano and guitar. Lean the guitar on the wall near the piano (not against it). Strike a piano key hard, let it sound for two seconds, then damp it. Listen carefully to the guitar. Try various keys. With certain notes, you hear the guitar strings vibrate too – as though plucked by an invisible guitarist. This is due to sympathetic resonance. Sound waves from the piano pass through the air, hit the guitar strings and make the string of the same note vibrate. Does the distance between piano and guitar alter the effect?

FAMOUS FIRSTS

THE GREAT ORGAN
Traditional pipe organs are found in many churches, concert halls and similar places. Sound is made by air blown through hollow pipes – both air and pipe vibrate. The pipes are resonators, used to enhance the notes. The bigger and longer the pipe, the deeper the note. The first pipe organs were mechanical versions of ancient pan pipes (see page 44).

DIY SCIENCE

PROOF OF SOUNDPROOFING
Specially designed materials absorb sound and keep it away from where it is not wanted. This is called soundproofing. Check everyday materials for their soundproofing qualities.

You need
Several identical cardboard boxes, loudspeaker, glue, sticking tape, scissors, test materials such as eggboxes, cardboard, foam plastic, newspaper, cotton wool, old rug or carpet.

DIY SCIENCE

ANALOGUE AND DIGITAL

A fretted instrument like the guitar illustrates the principle of a digital system. Different quantities - in this case, string lengths – fit into a set and prearranged scale, for example 1, 2, 3 centimetres and so on. An unfretted instrument like a cello (see photo), represents an analogue system. The quantities – in this case, string lengths again – can be anything from 0 upwards, in incredibly tiny steps. In theory there is endless variation. Try to copy a tune played by a cello on another cello and small differences could creep in. However the same process with the guitar, which has pre-made notes, is more likely to result in an exact copy.

Analogue type – card covers scale, so no pre-set divisions. You can press anywhere.

Digital type – divisions of scale work like frets, showing where to press the band

Make a 'digital' guitar (see page 23) with a scale showing where you press the rubber band, and an 'analogue' one where the scale is covered. Which is easier to play?

FASCINATING FACTS

- The noise from juggernaut trucks can shake and damage nearby structures such as buildings and bridges. The damage may come from sound waves through the air or from very low-frequency vibrations passing through the ground.

- The BA-Aerospatiale Concorde is the only passenger plane to fly faster than sound, at 2100 kph.

1. Line each box with the same thickness of a certain material, say 3 centimetres, carefully cut to size and glued or taped.

2. Place the loudspeaker on a flat surface on a carpet. Play a song or tune in which the sounds are fairly constant in volume.

3. Put the boxes one by one over the loudspeaker. Which makes it sound quietest? This material is best at absorbing sound waves.

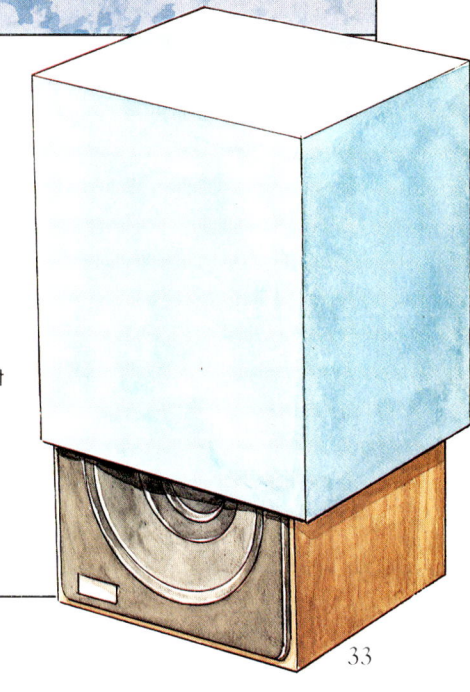

RECORDING SOUNDS

Recorded sound is part of life. We hear voices, music and other sounds which have been stored on discs, tapes and other equipment. We hear recorded sounds replayed on music systems, computers, televisions and radios. Yet around 100 years ago all sound was 'live'. It was produced at the time, by people talking, musicians, instruments and machines.

In the 1850s Alexander Bell senior devised a system of symbols called Visible Speech for sounds, not letters or words. It helped people with speech and hearing problems.

In 1877 British scientist John Strutt (Lord Rayleigh) published *The Theory of Sound*, which he wrote partly while staying in a houseboat on the River Nile in Egypt. The book collected and summarized the knowledge of the time about sound. It described the nature of sound waves, how they were made and how they travelled through various substances – from gases to metals. It predicted future research, laying the foundations for the science of acoustics.

The same year saw the start of recorded and played-back sound. It began with the words 'Mary had a little lamb'. Busy American inventor Thomas Edison and his machine-maker John Kreusi designed and made a new machine, called the phonograph. They had the idea while working on another device, a repeater to send on (or repeat) electrical telegraph messages. The phonograph was the first working device to record sounds in a physical form and play them back again. People were amazed by the invention. They could not believe that a machine could 'hear' what they said and then 'speak' it back to them, until they experienced the phonograph in action.

DIY SCIENCE

SOUNDS IN THE BRAIN

Close your eyes and imagine your favourite piece of music. It might be an orchestral piece or a rave beat. Try to remember all the details. Does it seem real? Now think of a close relative or friend. Imagine that they are speaking. Try to recall all the features of their pronunciation of words, which makes each voice seem unique. How do you do this? It does not happen in your ears, but in your brain – your 'mind's ear'. The human brain has an amazing ability to record many thousands of sounds as memories. It records not only the main features, but also the tiny details. This is how you know when someone is impersonating another person's voice. Even the best impressionists cannot copy voices exactly. When you hear a sound with your ears, and register it in your brain, you compare it at once with all the sounds stored in your memory banks. This is how you identify it. Like other memories such as sights, birth dates and word meanings, sound memories are probably stored as pathways through the billions of interlinked nerve cells in the brain. When a tiny electrical nerve signal flows around the pathway it activates the memory and you alone hear the sound in your mind.

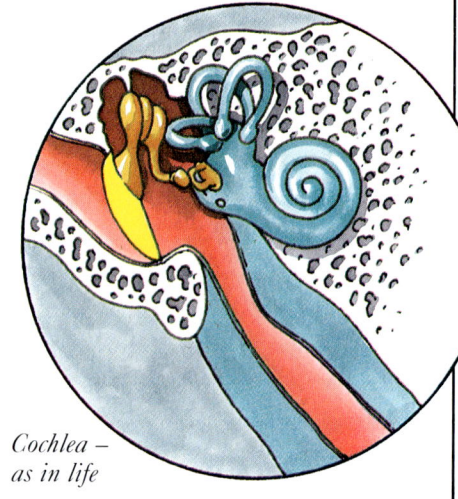

Cochlea – as in life

The tiny electrical nerve signals which represent sounds in the brain begin in the ear's cochlea (see page 26). In life, this is snail-shaped (above). Drawn in straightened form (below) it shows a long, flexible membrane. This vibrates in response to sounds and generates nerve signals which go along the auditory nerve to the brain.

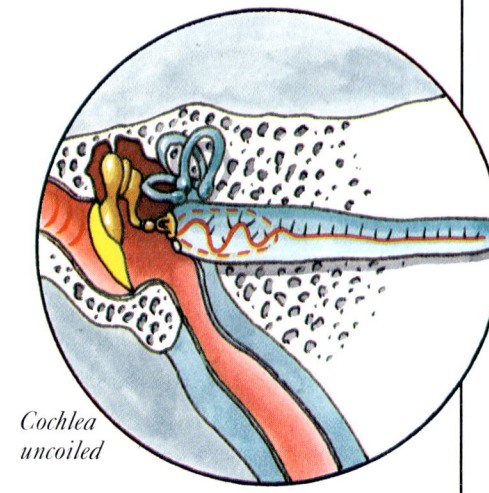

Cochlea uncoiled

SPECIAL FX

WORDS FOR SOUNDS

Hiss! Boo! Ugh! Words like these are written versions of sounds and noises which use the normal alphabet. The process of inventing words that sound like sounds, and using them in speech and writing, is called onomatopoeia. We have many onomatopoeic words, especially for animal sounds such as bark, miaow, baa and moo. Try writing a story containing as many of these words as possible.

SPECIAL FX

SOUNDS AND LETTER SHAPES

Look in a magazine or comic at the pictures, drawings and advertisements. You will usually see words with specially designed shapes, to make them look the way they sound. Often these are onomatopoeic words (see above). You could make up your own letter designs and word shapes, using extra lines, shading, stars and shapes, to emphasize the way the word should be pronounced.

FASCINATING FACTS

SIGNS FOR SPEECH

No other animals can copy the sounds of our own speech and understand its meaning – not even our nearest relatives, the chimpanzees. Although their voice-box and brain are not adapted to do this, chimps can learn to understand messages and 'speak' in a silent way, by sign language. They make signs with their hands and put together simple sentences such as 'Food me give!'

People communicate by sight, not sound, using the hand movements of sign language for letters, words and phrases. This is useful for people who cannot hear or speak clearly.

The original phonograph stored or recorded the sound in the form of a groove. This was pressed by a metal point, called a stylus, in a layer of tinfoil covering a brass cylinder. It was a mechanical system of moving parts and so it did not use any electricity.

Other inventors soon improved the quality of the recordings by replacing the foil with hard wax, in which the metal stylus cut a groove. In 1888 Emile Berliner introduced a flat disc instead of a cylinder. He also devised a method whereby the stylus moved from side to side, rather than up and down like Edison's original system. By 1904 Berliner had made an improved version that could be mass produced to a high-quality standard. The concept of the

The first tape-recorders of the 1930s had two separate large reels of wide tape and were very bulky. In 1980 the Sony Corporation introduced the first Walkman, which played compact cassettes. Anyone could then listen to recorded sound, anywhere they liked.

FAMOUS FIRSTS

EDISON'S PHONOGRAPH
The original phonograph both recorded sounds and played them back. Sound waves funnelled into the mouthpiece and bounced off a flexible thin-metal sheet, the diaphragm, making it vibrate. The diaphragm passed its vibrations to a steel needle, the stylus. This pressed a groove of varying depth in tinfoil covering a brass cylinder, which was being turned by hand. After a recording was made, the stylus was moved back to the start and the cylinder turned again. The process reversed and sent out sound waves from the funnel. One of the very first recordings was Edison reciting 'Mary had a little lamb'.

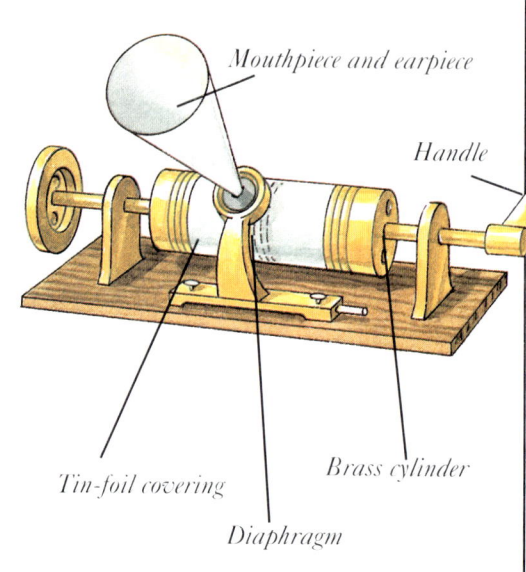

Mouthpiece and earpiece

Handle

Tin-foil covering

Diaphragm

Brass cylinder

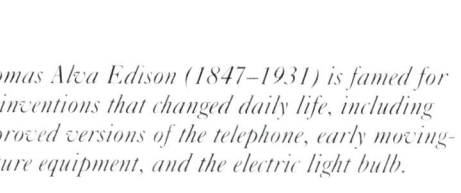

Thomas Alva Edison (1847–1931) is famed for his inventions that changed daily life, including improved versions of the telephone, early moving-picture equipment, and the electric light bulb.

FAMOUS FIRSTS

TAPE RECORDERS
The first system to store sound by using magnetism was invented by Vlademar Poulsen in about 1898 in Denmark. It used long, thin steel wire. The first tape machine was the German 'Magnetophon' of 1936. It used a flexible cellulose tape with a thin coat of magnetic powder. Philips sold cassettes in 1963. They were small and convenient, but not high-fidelity. Tapes with chrome coatings, and then other metal combinations, plus the Dolby noise-reduction system (see page 39), have much improved their quality.

OLD-TIME MUSIC

This home-made phonograph requires old 78 rpm records that are no longer needed. Carefully push a long-pointed drawing or mapping pin through the middle of the base of a thin plastic cup, so it sticks out below. Glue the pinhead to the cup base. Hold the cup rim by your fingertips and press the pinpoint at an angle on to the groove of the rotating record. The vibrations pass up the pin to the cup, which sends out sound waves.

Point of drawing pin

HEARING YOUR OWN VOICE

Sound waves from your voice-box are picked up by your ears. Voice-box vibrations also pass through the bones and flesh of your neck and head to your inner ears. So your ears receive two sets of vibrations from your voice compared to the single set of sound waves heard by others. This is why our recorded voice sounds different, because we hear one set of vibrations only. But it does not seem odd to other people, who always hear one set.

Place a microphone in different positions, like against your neck and skull, to record the different sounds of your voice.

FASCINATING FACTS

- Emile Berliner's first flat-disc records were made of hard rubber. This was followed by shellac, a resin-type substance originally obtained from certain insects. Eventually plastics were tried, including vinyl.

- Various improvements to the flat disc led to 10-inch and 12-inch diameter versions, rotating at 78 rpm (revolutions per minute).

- Longer periods of music and other sounds, over 30 minutes on each side of the disc, came in 1948 with the vinyl LP or long-playing record. Its 'microgrooves' were much thinner, and the disc went around slower, at 33 rpm.

- The single or 45, rotating at 45 rpm, had only a few minutes of sound recording on each side. But single records were cheap to make and many people could afford to buy them. This led to juke-box records in the 1940s and the best-seller lists of records, such as 'Top Ten' charts, from the 1950s.

12-inch LP (33 rpm)

10-inch record (78 rpm)

7-inch single (45 rpm)

'record' was born. During the early 1900s, the first commercial recordings were made of singers, musicians and speakers.

The invention of the triode valve to enlarge, or amplify, electrical signals meant that inventors could make sounds louder electrically (see page 24). Microphones and loudspeakers were developed and, in the 1920s, sound-recording systems changed from purely mechanical, to electrical. Gramophones, or record-players, found their way into many homes. Recorded sound became part of everyday life.

From the 1930s sound was also recorded as tiny patches of magnetism on flexible tape. The 1980s saw another form of recording arise – the compact disc. A CD's microscopic pits are read by a laser beam. Sounds are also stored in the form of magnetic patches in computer disks and in the solid-state 'chips' of computer memory circuits.

FAMOUS FIRSTS

The first movie films were 'silent'. This means there were no sounds recorded at the same time as the pictures. (Musicians in the cinema might play an accompaniment as the film was shown.) The first 'talkie' was *The Jazz Singer* starring Al Jolson, in 1927. Sounds were recorded at the same time as pictures and played back together. Jolson spoke and sang for part of the movie. The first film with complete accompanying sound, the soundtrack, was *Lights of New York* in the following year.

A scene from the first 'talkie', The Jazz Singer. Audiences were stunned to hear Jolson's voice, as though he was speaking to them from the screen. The silent film was dead within two years as the era of 'talkies' had begun.

Sounds are recorded on CD as microscopic pits in a layer of shiny metal, covered with transparent plastic for protection. A laser beam shines at the pits. The patterns of reflections are detected by a photo-sensor and turned into electrical signals.

Laser beam reflected

Sounds are recorded on tape as microscopic patches of magnetism on flexible tape coated with iron oxide. The patches are detected by electromagnetism (see page 22) as the tape slides past a coil of wire in the recording head, and turned into electrical signals.

Photo sensor

Laser emitter

Recording and playback head spins at speed.

Tape pillar guides

Magnetic tape

Digital Audio Tape

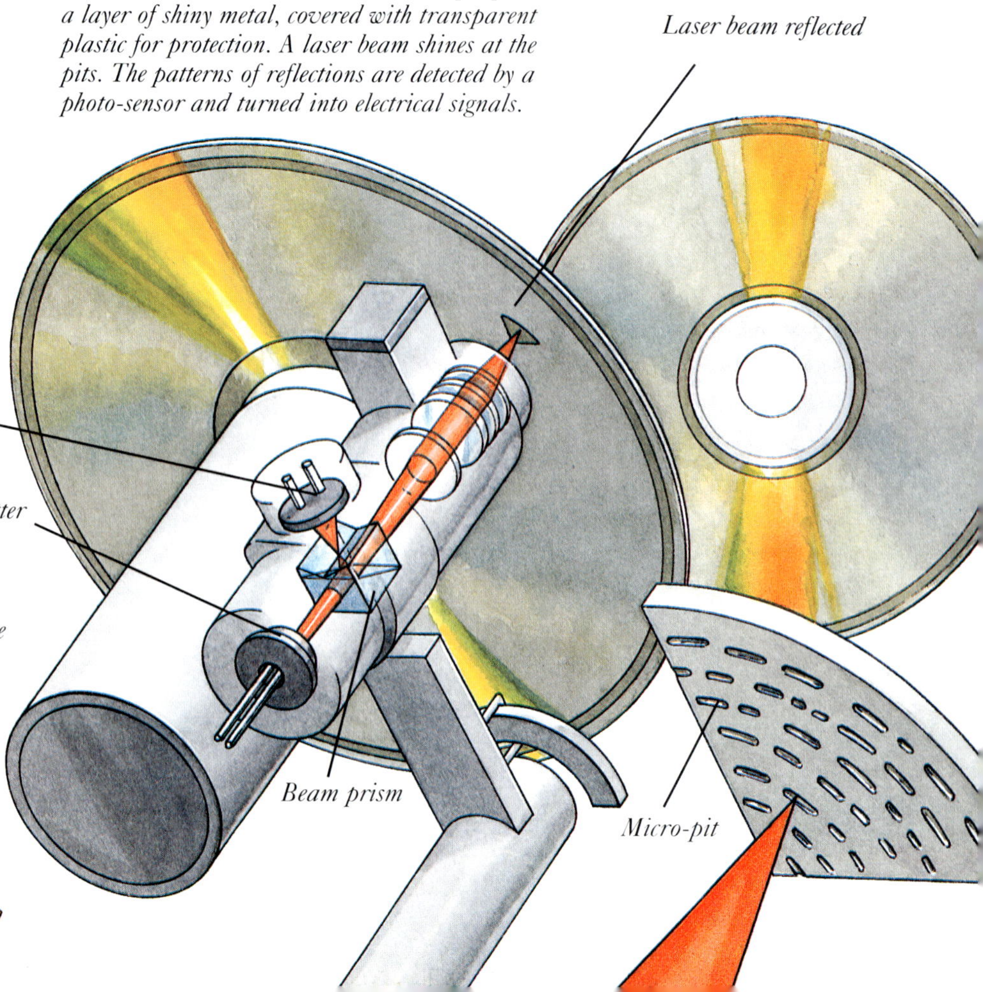

Beam prism

Micro-pit

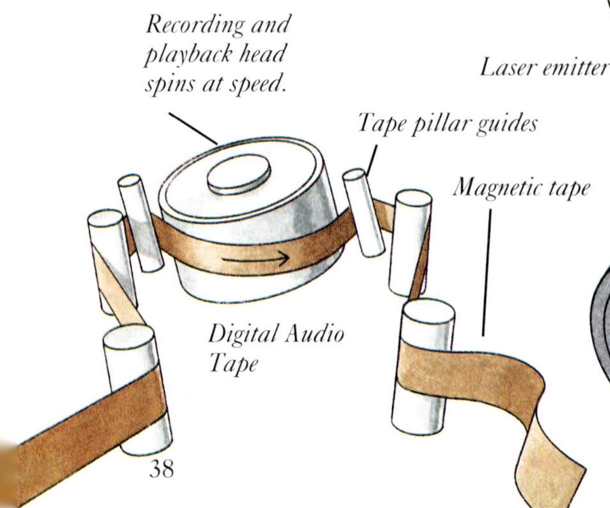

SIGHT AND SOUND

The sounds which accompany 'moving pictures' have been recorded in various ways. In 1894 Thomas Edison produced a simple system for playing back sounds from a phonograph, to accompany the pictures from his kinetoscope 'peep-show box'. In the 1920s the 'Vitaphone' worked in a similar way, with electrical signals to link or synchronize the movie film and the phonograph disc. Next, the sounds were converted into electrical signals, which were then turned into a pattern of light and dark pulses. These were recorded on the film itself next to the pictures, as a wavy stripe called an optical soundtrack. Videotape records the sound in the same form as it records pictures, as micro-patches of magnetism. Modern cine film also has a magnetic stripe along the side, to record the sound magnetically.

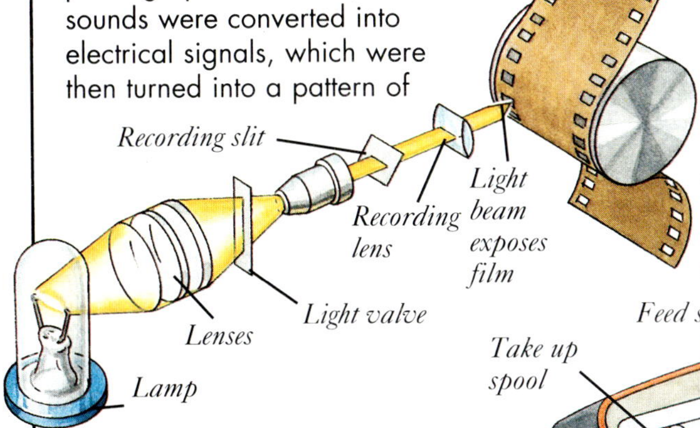

When movie frames are shown in a fast sequence, say 25 times per second, the eyes blur them into one continuous scene of movement.

Recording slit

Recording lens

Light beam exposes film

Light valve

Lenses

Lamp

Optical soundtrack recorder

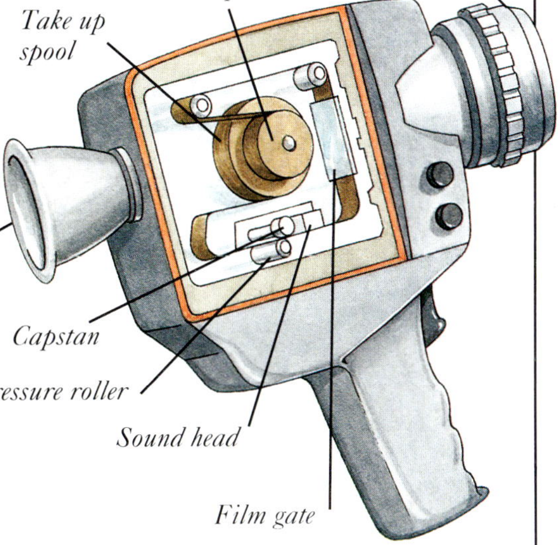

Feed spool

Take up spool

Lens

View finder

Super 8 home movie camera

Capstan

Pressure roller

Sound head

Film gate

Magnetic movie soundtrack player

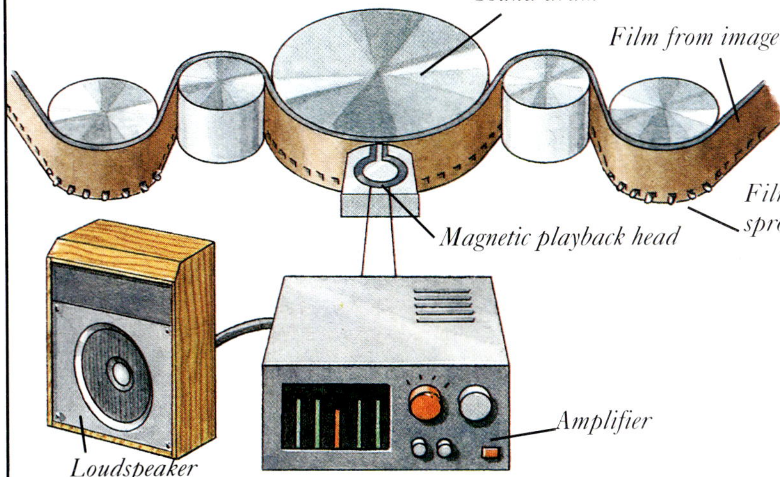

Sound drum

Film from image-projector

Magnetic playback head

Film drive sprocket

Amplifier

Loudspeaker

DOLBY® NOISE REDUCTION

The Dolby noise reduction system uses electronic circuits to improve sound quality, especially for cassette tapes. The system selects and boosts certain high frequencies, which often include background 'hiss'. It then filters and reduces these, and combines them with the rest of the sound. Dolby was devised in 1967 by American electrical engineer Ray Dolby. There are now several systems, including Dolby A, B, C and DBX, and Dolby Stereo for cinema soundtracks.

- In fibre-optic cables a voice on the telephone becomes coded as flashes of laser light. These pulse millions of times per second. Light travels more efficiently in long cables than electricity.

- In the 1880s Alexander Graham Bell worked on a fibre-optic device called the photophone, but it never became practical.

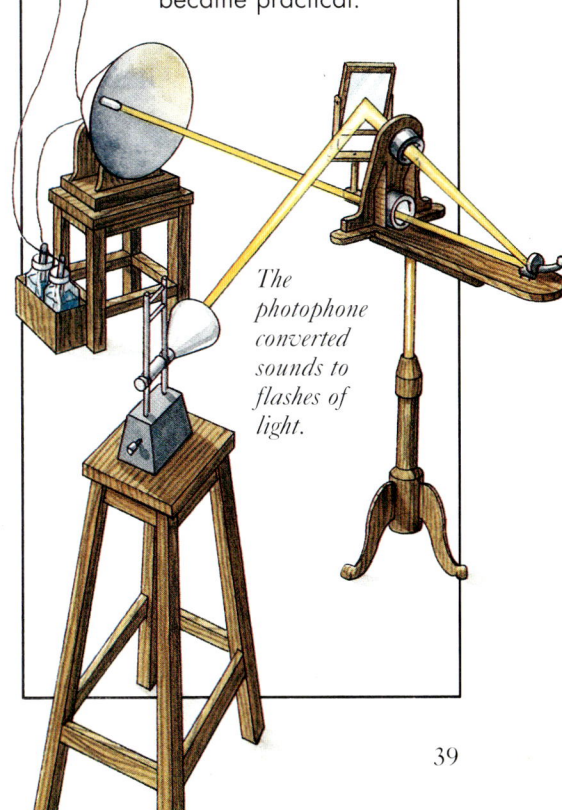

The photophone converted sounds to flashes of light.

39

USES FOR SOUND

Our lives are filled with sound. Through a typical day we may hear people talking, radios and televisions blaring, vehicles and machines working, music, wind and rain. Now and again we hear sounds that are out of the ordinary. They can make us startled, worried or even frightened. Other sounds can give us pleasure.

The baby's scream seems to pierce through you. Nature has designed its sound and our ears to be very sensitive to its cries, so that we respond and care for the baby.

It is a quiet, relaxing night in the countryside. The peace is shattered by a horrendous scream. Depending on the country, it may be a lion killing a gazelle or a fox killing a hare. Protected inside buildings we listen in the knowledge that we are quite safe. Yet humans have a long history living as part of nature. Alarming sounds still affect our instincts, making us nervous and edgy.

Throughout nature, animals use screams and wails to convey terror or aggression. They may be hunting their prey, fighting rivals for territories, repelling a predator, or trying to beat off competitors for mates to be able to reproduce. The sounds can be fearsome, even blood-curdling, and they are often coupled with visual displays of size and

Flashing lights are a visual warning. They are often accompanied by an auditory warning – the wail of a siren. If you cannot see one, you can usually hear the other.

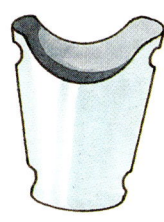

FASCINATING FACTS

ANIMAL ALARMS

Here are some of the alarm and warning sounds made by wild creatures. They may be a special version of the usual songs and calls made by that animal, using its voice-box. Or the sounds may be produced by special actions like hitting or stamping. Often they are combined with visual displays for greater effect. Other animals in the locality learn to respond as well, so one warning works for many.

A snake hisses to show that it may strike.

The toad hisses and puffs itself up to look bigger, if threatened by a predator.

A frightened cat hisses, bares its teeth, and makes its fur stand on end to look bigger.

Hisses are used as warnings by many types of animal, such as cats, snakes, toads and some insects and spiders. People use them to show suspicion or disapproval.

The gorilla shakes and rattles branches and may also beat its chest, to chase away rivals or intruders.

The rabbit stamps its back legs hard to make a thump that travels through the ground.

The beaver slaps its tail on the water's surface in alarm, such as sighting a wolf or cougar.

Slap, thrash and stamp – these sounds are made by an animal's actions, rather than by its voice-box. The beaver's tail-slap travels well through the water, to warn the rest of its family in the stream and pool near by.

The eagle is an airborne predator.

Ring-tailed lemurs live on the ground and in trees in Madagascar. If one lemur spots an aerial predator, it makes a certain alarm call, and the whole troop rushes to hide down on the ground. If it sees a ground predator, it makes another alarm call, and the troop knows to climb trees for safety.

Warnings like these are especially common among woodland animals. They cannot see each other or very far, through the tangle of trees, twigs and leaves, so visual signals are less useful. Woodland birds are particularly vocal.

The lemur changes its alarm call according to the type of predator.

strength. But if you make a warning noise, this is a relatively safe method of trying to scare an enemy or threaten a rival – at a distance. Once the confrontation gets to close quarters, with physical contact and combat, then the risks become far greater. Harm and injury are much more likely. In the wild this often leads to death. If animals can settle disputes by sight and sound rather than actual fighting, they usually do so.

The same kind of alarming sounds happen in the modern world of towns and cities. The wail of a siren, an aggressive shout and the cry of a frightened person are some of today's human equivalents of nature's warning sounds. They makes us alert, on edge and ready for action. These are some of the more unusual ways in which sounds have major effects on our

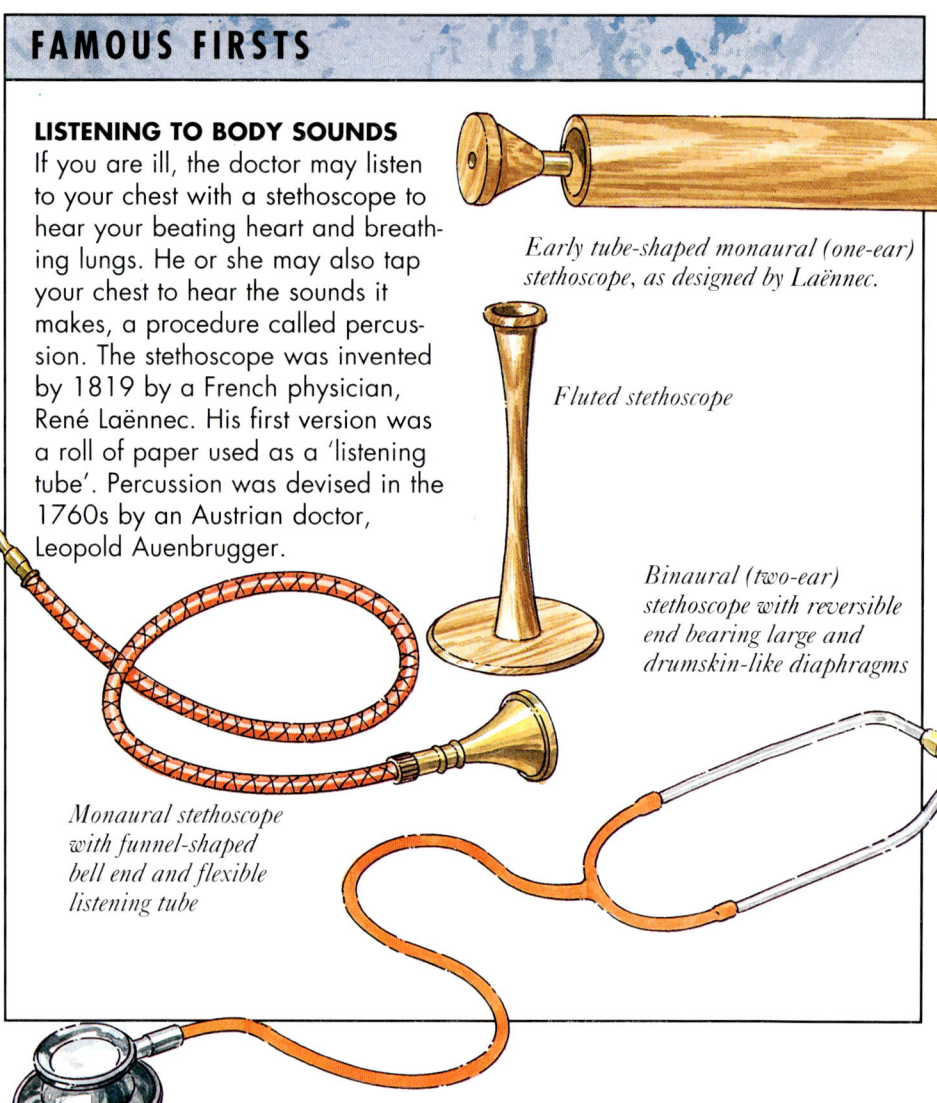

LISTENING TO BODY SOUNDS

If you are ill, the doctor may listen to your chest with a stethoscope to hear your beating heart and breathing lungs. He or she may also tap your chest to hear the sounds it makes, a procedure called percussion. The stethoscope was invented by 1819 by a French physician, René Laënnec. His first version was a roll of paper used as a 'listening tube'. Percussion was devised in the 1760s by an Austrian doctor, Leopold Auenbrugger.

Early tube-shaped monaural (one-ear) stethoscope, as designed by Laënnec.

Fluted stethoscope

Binaural (two-ear) stethoscope with reversible end bearing large and drumskin-like diaphragms

Monaural stethoscope with funnel-shaped bell end and flexible listening tube

The heart can be scanned by ultrasound using a technique called echocardiography. The resulting images are not as clear as other scanning techniques, such as CAT. But they have the advantage that they are real-time or 'live', and the doctors can watch the heart actually beating.

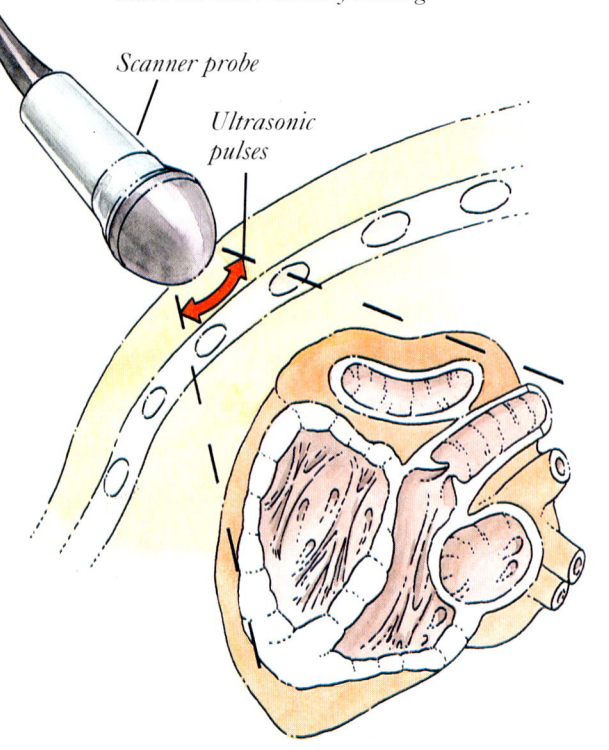

Scanner probe

Ultrasonic pulses

The ultrasound scan is a method of producing a picture of the inside of the body. Ultrasonic sound waves, too high-pitched for us to hear, are beamed into the body. Different parts such as bones, muscles and blood vessels reflect the waves in different ways. The reflections or echoes are picked up, processed by computer and the image displayed on a screen. Many expectant mothers are 'scanned' by ultrasound in early pregnancy, to check the baby is healthy. Ultrasound can also detect growths, tumours and other abnormalities.

Ultrasound scan of a baby in the womb after 16–18 weeks of pregnancy.

Echocardiogram of a living, beating heart. The main heart chambers are on the left.

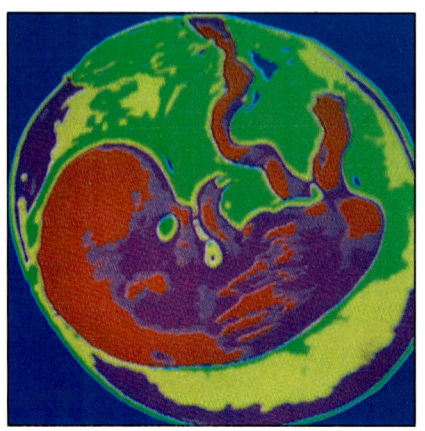

HEAR YOUR HEARTBEAT

When Laënnec invented the stethoscope, as described on the left, he improved the paper roll into a wooden tube. One end was placed on the patient's chest, and the other to the doctor's ear. The modern stethoscope usually has a bell-end, covered by a thin, flexible diaphragm (membrane), and hollow listening tubes leading to two ear pieces. But Laënnec's simple design still works well, as you can hear for yourself.

You need

Plastic funnel, plastic tube or hose, friendly 'patient', adult supervision.

1. Push one end of the plastic tube over the thin end of the funnel, to make a good seal. This is the stethoscope.

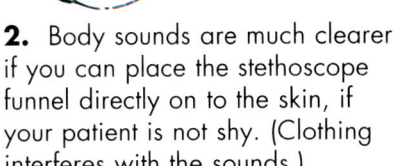

2. Body sounds are much clearer if you can place the stethoscope funnel directly on to the skin, if your patient is not shy. (Clothing interferes with the sounds.)

3. Listen carefully with the hearing end to your ear, and the funnel end on different parts of the chest. Can you hear the heart beating and the air whooshing in and out of the lungs?

THE ECHO SOUNDS OF SONAR

Sound travels fast and far through water. Sonar – SOund NAvigation and Ranging – uses it to locate and identify objects, from the sea bed to a shoal of fish or an enemy submarine. Sonar works like radar, but with sound waves instead of radio waves. Sound pulses bounce off objects, hydrophones (underwater microphones) detect the echoes, and a computer analyses the results. An early sonar system was developed by French scientist Paul Langevin in 1915, for ships to detect icebergs. It was much improved after World War I, after the threat of German U-boats (submarines), to detect enemy submarines in future conflicts. Some types of sonar are called echo-sounders.

Range 10 kilometres or more

Computer analyses strength and time delay of echoes

Sound echoes received by hydrophone

Sound pulses reflect from object

Sonar pulses sweep to and fro across the sea bed.

- In the deep ocean, the sperm whale uses sound to stun or kill its prey. It sends out giant grunts, immensely powerful bursts of sound that can disable nearby fish, squid and other victims.

- In the middle of the night, an eerie tap-tap-tap in an old building was thought to be a ghost or spirit, come to take away the living, or return with the souls of the dead. In fact, it is the death-watch beetle banging its jaws and head on the wood. The tapping sound is its call for a mating partner. The beetle's grubs tunnel into oak trees and old oak beams in houses.

In a large chorus or choir, people are grouped according to the singing pitches of their voices. From high to low, and front to back, a simplified system of this is treble (boys and girls), soprano (high female), contralto (low female), alto (high male), tenor (medium male), baritone (deeper male) and bass (deepest male).

minds and bodies. They alert us and warn us of possible danger.

Sounds can have exactly the opposite effect, too – usually in the form of music. Different instruments and styles of music can put us in different moods. A slow, soft song soothes and relaxes, while a fast, loud one brings out energy and action. To stimulate our ears the music studio, television set, radio room, disco club and the concert hall contain masses of microphones and wires, arrays of switches and controls, and banks of loud-speakers. Yet sounds can be much simpler and just as pleasurable. We sing along with friends, cheer our heroes, and laugh and cry together. In every way sound and its science is a vital part of our lives.

SPECIAL FX

SINGING FOR REAL
Most people can warble some words or trill a tune. But high-quality singing, as in classical music or opera, needs practice and advice from a coach or teacher. One important feature is to 'sing from deep down' in the body. This means using the diaphragm and abdominal (belly) muscles to help the chest blow air from the lungs, through the voice-box. If you use the chest or neck muscles alone, the voice sounds tight, shallow and 'strangled' – and you soon run out of breath.

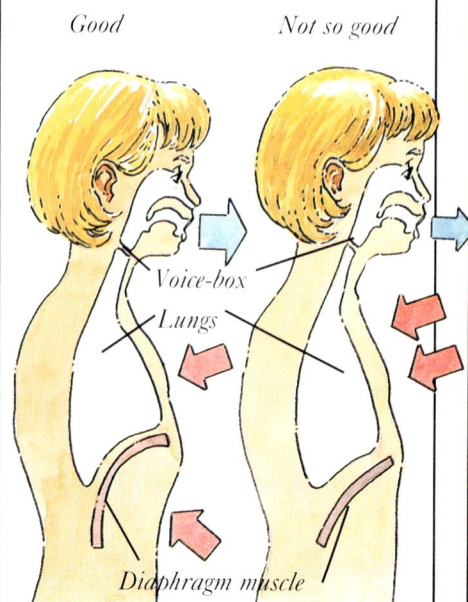

Good *Not so good*

Voice-box
Lungs

Diaphragm muscle

SPECIAL FX

PAN'S PIPES
Pan was a Greek god of animals known for his soothing music.

You need
Bamboo or wooden tubes, sticking tape, modelling clay, scissors or small saw, adult supervision.

1. Stopper one end of the tube with clay. Place the other end to your lower lip and blow gently across the opening to make the pipe vibrate and sound a note.

2. Trim some tubes shorter for higher notes. Adjust the lengths until the tubes make a musical scale when blown one by one. Tape them in a row and play.

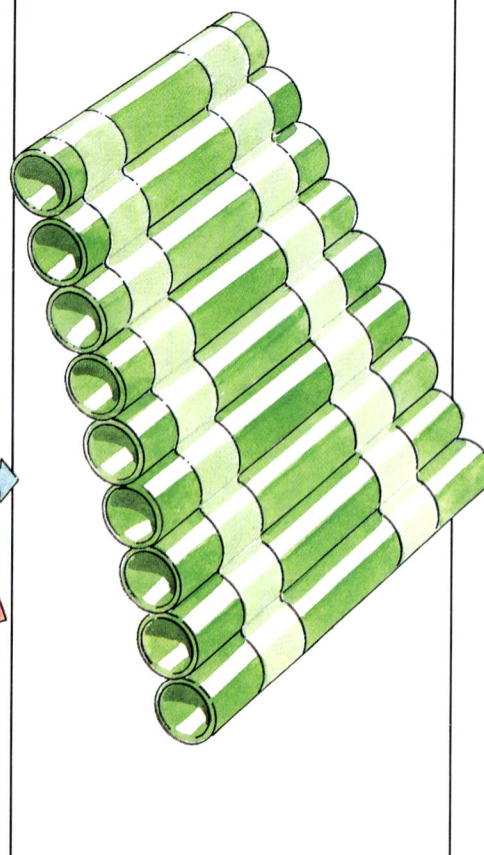

SOUNDS MUSICAL

Most of us know when sounds are 'music' rather than 'noise'. We can hear distinct notes of certain pitches that go together, and the sounds have a pleasing quality and blend well. The usual Western musical scale goes up in sets of eight main notes, called octaves: 'do, ray, me, far, so, la, tee, do'. Written music uses sets of five lines, the staves. Going up these indicates a higher pitch or frequency of a note. The notes are written as duration symbols to show how long they should last. Other signs and words indicate the speed, type of rhythm, loudness and other features of the music.

○ *Semibreve*

♩ *Minim*

♩ *Crotchet*

♪ *Quaver*

♫ *Semi-quaver*

Treble clef E F G A B C D E

Basic notes on a musical stave and how they translate to a piano keyboard.

Basic notes on guitar strings

Sixth and thickest string

E   F   G   A   B   C   D

First and thinnest string   *Open string*   *Place finger here*

FASCINATING FACTS

- Acoustics play a large part in the design of modern concert halls, theatres and similar buildings. The travels of a sound wave can be shown on a computer screen, for different frequencies and volumes of sound, for varying shapes of the hall's interior and for different materials covering them. This is why many such buildings have strange shapes on the walls and ceiling, such as discs, panels and saucers, to absorb or reflect the sounds.

- Huge cathedrals, with their hard walls and floors of stone, glass and wood, are amazing places for acoustics. Almost any sound seems loud and long, as it echoes and reverberates through the huge air space and bounces off the surfaces. This is why church singing sounds so special.

- In a recording studio any stray sound is a nuisance. So the walls, ceilings and floors are covered with sound-absorbing substances, such as wavy-surfaced tiles and thick carpets. There is a continuing search for 'acoustically dead' materials that absorb all sounds.

The spectacular shapes above this concert stage help to add to the visual effect. But they are really to improve the auditory quality, to direct sound waves so that the audience hears the singing and music most clearly.

INDEX